MORE BLACK COUNTRY FOLK AT WERK

NED WILLIAMS

Ned Williams

Dolly Allen	Clarry Siviter
Geoff Cartwright	Les Clough
Bob Hosier	Ena Walden
George and Betty Salt	Edna Smart
Derek Simmonds	Sylvia Shaw
Jan Bruton	Ethel Barlow
Billy Kayes	Jack Haden
George Reohorn	Albert Booth
Joe Davis	Dennis Whitehouse
Winnie Large	Lily Tighe
Amy Davies	John Guttery
Phyllis Rudd	Edna Micklewright
John Spittle	Bill Harris
Steral Williams	Archie Clarke
Ken Souhtern	Charles Wyatt
Jack Winship	Joe Ashton
Arthur James	Cecil Westwood
Horace Hodgekiss	Vera Hodgekiss
Bert Wootton	Alf Bridgwood
Ted Tonks	Cecil Perry
Bert Bradford	Ken Allen

URALIA PRESS

23 WESTLAND ROAD   WOLVERHAMPTON WV3 9NZ

Learning to work: Left: Brian Paddock cleaning swarf from castings at Conex Sambra in 1954. Right: Pam Kaur working on a CNC lathe while on a womens' technician course at Wulfrun College 1988. (Photos: BCS collection and Simon Larson, Wulfrun College)

The picture on the front cover shows Dorothy Millward at her Hoffman Press at the Wolverhampton Steam Laundry. As you will see on page 50, long service is a tradition at the steam laundry. Dorothy has worked there about thirty years. The laundry itself celebrates its centenary as we go to press in 1990. (Photo: Jonathan Lewis)

More Black Country Folk at
Werk
Ned Williams
Uralia Press 1990

ISBN 0 9511223 5 5

Design: John Revill
Photo printing: Jan Endean
Photo screening: Brian Homer with Andy and Charlotte

Printed in the Black Country by
Gibbons Barford Print, Wolverhampton

CONTENTS

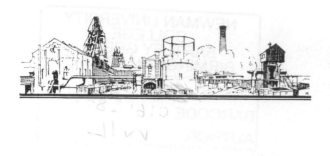

INTRODUCTION

Welcome to *More Black Country Folk at Werk*: a sequel to *Black Country Folk at Werk*, published a year ago in Autumn 1989. Once again local people give you a picture of their working lives - in their own words.

Even before the first of these two books was published, I was aware that it was not possible to present a comprehensive account of local people's experience of work within the pages of one book covering less than fifty occupations. Now that it is possible to present further accounts, I still do not think it is possible to claim "comprehensiveness". However many pieces are added to the jig-saw, the picture will never be complete, but somehow that does not seem to invalidate the task of collecting the pieces.

Perhaps my own pleasure in collecting this material has been the main factor that has led to publishing this book. On the other hand, I have been encouraged by the willingness of many contributors to take part. The task of creating a book like this is made into a pleasure precisely because of the generosity with which people share their memories.

Last year's anthology tried to be logical in its structure in that the first accounts came from folk who had worked in the coal trades, then the iron and steel trades, then via the well-known manufacturing trades of the Black Country, through to accounts of work in the service industries, transport and retailing. A second volume might logically set out to fill in some of the omissions, but it has not quite worked out like that. Firstly, the Black Country itself tends to defy logic. In fact, a characteristic of the area is its capacity for surprises! Secondly, there are some omissions that are very difficult to cover. For example, it is very difficult to find an account of work in the area of domestic service, or in the area of agriculture, that definitely existed within the Black Country until so recently.

To a large extent the accounts presented here are a personal selection - exploring areas of work that for one reason or another have interested me, while, at the same time, hopefully providing insights and new surprises for the reader. Having said that, there are various balances I have tried to observe. For example, I have tried to include stories from all quarters of the Black Country - not just the north western boundary area in which I live and work! Within the four Metropolitan Boroughs of Wolverhampton, Walsall, Dudley, and Sandwell, lies the vast sprawling network of industrialised towns and villages we call the Black

Above: Black Countryman at work: Harry Peach glueing cores together at Sandwell Castings in October 1954. Harry started working for the company in 1936, and his "finished" cores can be seen in the left foreground. Core-making is a traditional skill associated with the Black country's foundry industry. (BCS collection)

Country. To me, as a car-driver of the 1990's, it is one region, but I realise that many Black Country folk have lived and worked within much more localised horizons.

In the past, someone who lived in Darlaston probably worked for one of the large employers in that town, or, in search of work, or for social reasons, may have ventured to Walsall or Wednesbury. But I realise that they may never have crossed "the bonk" to enjoy the wonders of Cradley Heath or Quarry Bank. Since the War, accompanied by the rise of private transport, the "journey-to-work" pattern of travel in the Black Country has become incredibly complex, but that has not destroyed strong local feelings of identity. The problem is to find descriptions of work that celebrate that local individuality, while, at the same time, clearly contribute to our feeling of belonging to the Black Country region. It is, therefore, very fitting to begin this book with the words of the late Dolly Allen. Dolly came from Halesowen, and worked for Hackett's for forty years. Her career in entertainment began exclusively in the south western corner of the Black Country, yet once she became well known she seemed to represent the whole of the region. I hope the accounts in this book perform the same trick, managing to be very individual and very local, but at the same time incorporating the special quality that can be recognised in peoples' lives from Walsall to Wombourne, and from Sodom to Paradise.

Right: The popular image of the working environment in Industrial Britain: a machine shop - a clean, bright, well-lit space in which men in overalls bend over lathes. This picture was taken at Conex Sambra, Tipton, in the 1950's. It is the kind of scene immortalised by the opening sequence of the 1962 film, "Saturday Night & Sunday Morning", featuring Albert Finney in the Raleigh factory at Nottingham. That's the point - machine shops look much the same in any part of Britain, and still exist today although computer controlled machines are now at work. The individuality of the Black Country is better represented by its foundries, forges, lock works, trap works, chain shops etc.

It may seem perverse to present a portrait of work in the Black Country by commencing with "Show Business" but of course the comedienne was a press operator in a nut and bolt factory by day, and the drummmer in the local dance band drove a crane in the foundry. Industry wasd never far away. Jan Bruton' account of the cinema at Brierley Hill is overshadowed by the neighbouring steel works, and as you will see, the manager had to halt the show one afternoon in order to "dust the patrons". Pits, ironworks, foundries and factories made the Black Country "black", and the dust and grime were never far away. In this book we take a look at the laundry and dry cleaning trade to attempt a symbolic escape from the "blackness", creating an opportunity for you to mentally compare the lives and work of the folk in the laundry with the lives and work of the folk in the iron foundry.

"Black Country Folk at Werk" ended with a glimpse of Wednesbury folk out in the countryside - not escaping from the "blackness" to some rural idyll, but taking on seasonal work in the hop fields. In this book several hop-pickers share their memories of the task. As they headed for the border of Worcestershire and Herefordshire they left the pits and ironworks behind, but they took a little of the Black Country with them, and stayed together in groups recruited from their own locality. Just occasionally they compared notes. For example most hop-pickers experienced "trouble" from the education authorities back home, but note the Walsall hop-picker who compares his lot with the folk from Cradley Heath, and decides, "The Education Committee people ought to be burnt."

Some occupational groups seem better story-tellers than others, and I always find that transport workers are good communicators - that's why I make no excuse for including their accounts once again. In other sections of the book you may find my own interests surfacing - but that is partly because so many things do "criss-cross" in the Black Country. For example, I went to see George Reohorn as a result of my interest in Pat Collins and his fair. George's father was Lump Coal Billy, one of Pat's traction engine drivers, but I came away from the interview with a fascinating account of working in the Fire Service from George himself.

Work in the industrial and manufacturing sector appears in the final section of the book. Having worked alongside engineers for over twenty years, I must confess that I find their world relatively impenetrable! As I listen to their accounts of their working lives I sometimes find it very difficult to picture the process they are describing. I hope I have enabled their words to be understood here, because, having consigned them to the back of the book, I am by no means denying their importance in shaping the Black Country. I am glad I am old enough to have been down the pit on several occasions, to have worked briefly at both Round Oak and Bilston Steel Works, to have been in traditional foundries and rolling mills. However, I realise that such experiences are becoming part of the past and that a generation will come along without any sense of the "blackness" of the Black Country.

As industry built the Black Country and transformed the landscape, people were dragged into the area from all over the place. As a "furriner" myself, I suppose I find immigration an interesting aspect of living in such an area, and I am pleased to hear about it when listening to the accounts of peoples' working lives - see the stories of Joe Davies and Ken Southern. Now that we have all arrived in the Black Country, and industry, as we have known it, has departed, we seem to face a new problem of defining the Black Country, and deciding what we are doing here!

This book does not answer those questions, but it does give us the chance to flick through the pages and share some reflections on the immediate past - share our experience of working in the Black Country. That process of sharing the experience affects me, as the compiler of the book, very strongly. I am often over-whelmed by peoples' generosity as they give me their time, mental energy, and artefacts, as we sit down together to talk about "werk". I hope the generosity of that act of sharing experience is something that communicates itself clearly to the reader. I hope the humour, the interest in recalling detail, the very personal quality of the words of the contributors makes it as interesting for you to read as it has been for me to compile.

As stated in "volume one", this book is an attempt to counterbalance the trend towards presentation of recent history in purely visual terms. This book is presented in the belief that people's *words* are important. However, if you felt you would have liked more pictures in last year's book, you will be pleased to see that this volume does include a greater proportion of pictures. There are no pictures in this book that are simply lifted from local libraries or archives. Work is not an aspect of people's lives that they have usually stopped to photograph. Therefore, despite the importance of the text itself, I do feel the pictures in this book are "gems", and I hope you share my excitement in looking at a picture from someone's private collection, that has probably never been published before.

Words and pictures relating to all the many aspects of life in the Black Country are worth preserving. When we meet people, we understand them better if they reveal something of their past, and it is the same with a place: to enrich our understanding of this place called the Black Country we need to know a little about its past.

Words and pictures relating to all the many aspects of the Black Country are worth preserving. When we meet new people, we understand them better if they reveal something of their past, and it is the same with a place: to enrich our understanding of this place called the Black Country, we need to know a little about its past. One method of "knowing" is to race to the bookshelf and archive. Another method is to grab a notebook, camera, tape recorder or sketchpad, and talk to everyone you meet and everybody they send you off to see next. This book is created by the latter approach — obviously it is an approach that comes with my recommendation.

Enjoy the book — enjoy the Black Country.

Ned Williams
Autumn 1990.

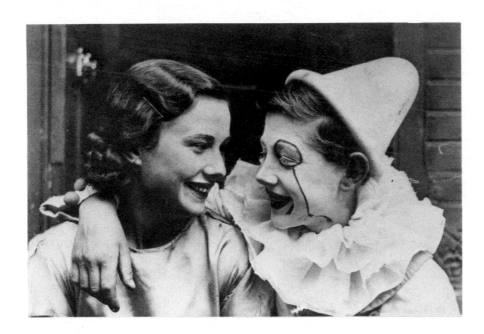

Left: Another face of Black Country "werk". Colliers, iron makers, metal bashers etc. all sought entertainment in their limited leisure time. Fairs, circuses, variety theatres, cinemas etc. provided that entertainment and created work of their own. Nora and Billy Kayes first came to the Black Country as part of their father's circus that travelled with Pat Collins' fair at the end of the end of the 1930s. (See page 20) (Nora Collins' collection)

Acknowledgements

I am always grateful for suggestions and particular introductions that lead to the collection of each memoir, and in this respect I would like to thank Peter Thurley, Alma Rudd, June Miller, Stan Hayes, June Wheeler of the Express & Star, Alan Butler, Lillian Sheldon, and probably many others, including the contributors themselves.

Photographic assistance has been given by Nick Hedges, May Griffiths, Ann Thomas, Cyril Hand, Rosemary Morrell, Stan Wilkins and, again, many of the contributors. Jan Endean has processed most of the photographs for me, and Peter Eardley has encouraged me with his supportive interest in this task. Dave Whyley has once again made available the resources of the Black Country Society's photographic collection, and I am pleased the Express & Star have allowed me to use their photographs. If no acknowledgement appears at the end of a caption it is because I have taken the picture myself, or it is from my own collection. Local libraries and archives have been most helpful.

During the production of this book many people have played a part. John Revill has again tried to make my work conform to some of the principles of graphic design, and has put in a great deal of his time in doing so. Juliet Thompson has corrected the proofs and Mark has assisted with the type setting. The folks at Galata Print have always assisted me with the production of last minute art work.

1

SHOWBUSINESS

Dolly Allen

Hullo my luvvers, this is Dolly Allen,

At school, when I was about eight years of age, if it was raining they used to let us stop in the corridors, where the hot pipes ran along close to the floor. We used to sit on the pipes in the corridors where we used to hang our coats. All of a sudden, while we were sitting there one day, laughing and joking, I don't know why, I just got up and started to dance. All the children enjoyed it so much, I began making plans for the next rainy day.

When the next rainy day came along I had already picked a song that I was going to sing to them. I sang a song that's years old now: "I want to telephone to Mother Dear". While I was singing I did not know that the Headmaster was standing at the back listening to me. After I had finished he clapped and said, "Very good, I'll give you a penny for singing that." And that penny was more to me than if I was to be given £50 today, because in them days a penny was so much. You could pick your own sweets for a halfpenny, you could even have a lollypop for a halfpenny - so a penny was lovely.

One day I joined the Band of Hope. They had a stage in one of the places where we met - in the old fashioned Cong's Hall in Hagley Road, Halesowen. Everybody in my age group would remember that place. We met there about once a week, and one or another of us would climb on the stage and do a turn. When I went on I used to sing and dance, just like I did at school.

One important event in my life was the Talent Contest at the Borough Hall, where Sidney Bray showed pictures and put on shows. We were all there on a Saturday afternoon - it used to be packed. It only cost a halfpenny to go in, and for that you sometimes came out with an orange, so what profit Sidney Bray made out of that lot, I don't know.

Bray was ever so good with the children. He got on the stage and said, "Now children, this aftrenoon I am going to give you a treat - I want six of you to get onto the stage, and sing, dance or recite. The winner will be given sixpence." Of course, everybody wanted to get on stage when they heard that. He picked six of us and I was the second to perform.

Above: Dolly Allen, as she will be remembered by most Black Country folk. Her costume and props did change over the years, but since appearing in the "Black Country Night Out" shows her image became fixed in this form, also immortalised on the sleeve of her long playing record. Her costume, style and dead-pan delivery created the impression that one was being spontaneously harangued by a lady in the bus queue, but her monologues were rigorously composed and committed to memory - Dolly was "putting on a show".

The First World War had just finished, and I knew a song that had come out during that War. I sang it, doing all the actions to it, shooting a gun and everything. And thus it went on until all six had performed. The lad before me had sung, "My Heart is as Light as a Feather - I Hope It Will Never Grow Sad!" I've never forgotten his words, because he came nowhere! Bray stood on the stage again and said, "Now children, I want you to to be the judges - which one of the six was the best?" They all shouted, "'Er! 'er what a bin doin' them things like that with the gun!" Bray was putting variety on at the Borough Hall, and one of the artistes presented me with the sixpence.

When I went up the road with that sixpence, I felt everyone was looking at me. I felt above six foot high. I went back home, but before I went into Mother's, I went over the road to see the woman that Mother knocked about with. I was that proud I said, "Look what I've won, Fanny!", and she says, "Ahhrr - your Mother won't half be glad when she sees that."

I went home, and said, "Mother, look what I've won." "Gerron. Yo'aven't." She went on, "Fanny owed me sixpence, and I've just sid you comin' in from Fanny's. She's given you that sixpence." It took me ages to

7

Above: Dolly Allen, much earlier in her career - having established her act as part of Harry Hatton's shows in the Lye, but still only known, at that time, in the south western corner of the Black Country.

convince her that I had won it, and then she came out with:

"Well now, we've got no coal - so with that sixpence yo' can go and fetch a quarter!"

"Oh Mother," I said, "I want that sixpence for myself." But it was no good. I had to go to the end of the road to get a quarter of coal. They lent me a dobbin - a big thick one with long 'ondles. I had to wheel it back, and you could hear it coming half way up the road, with its cast iron wheels. Mother came down the road to meet me.

"Oh Mother, look what I've had to do for a tanner." "Never mind," she says, "Yo'll 'ave a nice warm from the fire." So I had to tip the coal out, and cart the dobbin all the way back - and walk home again - all that lot for winning a tanner. I thought to myself, "I hope I never win another!"

Despite this incident, I had a happy childhood, and my foster parents were as good as gold - I might not have been treated as well if I'd had my proper parents. My real Mother had died giving birth to me, and I was adopted when I was three. That is my earliest memory - the moment when my foster mother came for me, I can still see that moment now. When I look back I feel I've had marvellous times - that's why I can put my Black Country together, and bring in things that perhaps other people have forgotten.

When I left school I started work at Hackett Brothers, the Nut and Bolt factory. The name went back to when the business had started - not the people who owned it while I was there. They were supposed to have the largest anvils in Halesowen. I reckon the men at Hacketts really worked hard, and there was that much subbing going on that they virtually picked up nothing at the end of the week. I met the man who became my husband there.

I used to sit in a corner on my own - all the other girls were working farther up the shop, and this gave me a chance to be alone and think. I was sitting by my press one day, carrying on with my work, when I thought, "I've a good mind to compose while I am sitting here."

The first one I composed was, "The Coal Pickin'", based on my experience of a very bad coal strike. Four or five of us had gone onto the Hawne Bank, and that's where I started coal pickin'. We did have some fun, and the experience was something I could bring into my composition. All my life I've tried to bring memories into my compositions that should be kept for posterity. I hoped that people could hear the poem and imagine how we used to come up with the dobbins. I changed it, saying that when I got married I brought my husband into the coal pickin' - that made it into a good joke, and we used to go down to Stratford from Halesowen in brakes. I went with my Mother, and memories of that kind of thing came back to me as I sat at my press. I sat there composing these verses, but I never wrote them down. As I composed a verse, I'd go back through it again in my head to memorize it, and then start the next verse. When I come to think of it now, I wonder how I remembered them right through from the beginning to the end, but I could. Mind you, I almost went crackers going over the verses again and again in my mind. Even when I picked up my nuts, and I had to count them into a bag, there was many a time I forgot what I was doing. I was concentrating so much on composing.

Some my earliest performances of these compositions were at the Works Suppers. The first monologue that I composed for them was about the work. It was a good laugh, but I can only remember parts of it now because people wouldn't be bothered to hear about me starting work. At any party I went to they would always ask me to say it again - and they liked the parts where I named the people I worked with.

My son, Ken Allen, became a singer. He had a marvellous voice, and he also started at the Borough Hall when he was eight. They produced tickets with his name on, and on the night there was a huge queue from the Borough Hall to the end of Grammar School Lane, longer even than for the pictures. He has loved singing and going on stage all his life.

Harry Hatton, from the Lye, used to present "Local Discoveries". The shows were put on at the Lye Church Hall, opposite the Vic. He had heard about Ken, and asked him to do a show for him. Ken did so, and it went down well. My husband said to Harry, "You ought to hear 'er, with 'er monologues - I daresay some 'll like it!" So it was agreed that I should go on. When I met Harry Hatton, on the day after the show, he said, "Yo've bin the talk of the Lye!" I thought he meant scandle or something like that. "They loved it last night — Yo've bin the talk of the place." From then on he used to include me in the show once every month, and coaches used to bring folk from Halesowen to see us. We could gaurantee a full house for ages with just us on - me, Ken, and three young girl singers. It went on until Harry Hatton was too ill to keep the shows going.

Outsiders had seen me by then, and I got letters from them asking if would go and entertain them at their clubs, and that went on until I joined Ray Hingley's

"Black Country Night Out". At one time there had only been three Black Country comedians - and I think if we hadn't carried on, it would have died out. There was Enoch Hackett, and there were Tommy Smith and Harry Bissell who did a double act, and there was me - I think I was the only Black Country woman comedian around. We performed mainly in the clubs, mainly around Halesowen, but we branched out as far as Cradley Heath, and up to Dudley. It seems strange that we now take Black Country humour anywhere.

I joined Ray Hingley after seeing an advert in the Black Country Bugle one day, and I wrote to Harry Harrison asking if I could join them. Ray was sent over to see what I was like, and invited me to join them, and I've been with them for sixteen years. I don't write new material, I just keep everything in my head, apart from writing down a new joke when I hear one. I bring these jokes in when I can, and change them when I get fed up with saying them, and that's how I go on. My son used to ask me to write my compositions down, but now I've made a record of them, for Jon Raven, and I think we've sold about forty thousand copies! My favourite verse is the one about my husband "on the Labour" but I'm also pretty fond of the first monologue I composed about my courting - composed while I worked with those big iron plates - making the nuts that go on gas pipes. Although I left briefly just once, I worked at Hacketts for forty years, making nuts and composing Black Country verse.

Dolly Allen died on 25 June 1990 after a short illness. Her act was presented for the last time on 12 April. Her son, Ken Allen, agreed that her contribution to this book should be published as planned, and has been able to say a little more about Dolly's "other" working life, and the part played in all the family's lives by the firm of Hackett Brothers.

Ken Allen: I think my Grandad Francis, and Uncle Will, were the first members of the family to work for Hackett Brothers. They worked in the nail shops. Then my father, Leonard Allen, worked there, and his brother Horace.

My mother, Dolly, worked there, and finally I joined the company. Dad started on the block, but elevated himself to heading tool setter, which is what I eventually became.

Dolly originally worked in the screwing shop, putting the threads on the bolts, and went from there into the press shop. In there, her job was cutting the big hexagon-shaped "gas" nuts from plates that had to pushed under the unguarded press. There was always a risk that if the tool broke, you could be blinded, or have your fingers cut off, but she liked the work, and became so used to it that she was able to compose the monologues as she worked. She was very good at the job and was a hard worker. Dolly later worked on a nut-forming machine, in the shop where I was working. I was a setter/operator, and she operated. It wasn't a light job, and it wasn't an easy job for a woman, but she liked it.

There were other very distant relations working in the making of nails, and there were other families to be found there - it was a very "family" factory. Before the War they held a big party every Christmas, and there were annual coach trips, but these dropped away during the War. Halesowen people were tempted to work for higher wages at the Austin during the War, and many preferred to catch the train to Longbridge rather than work at factories like Hackett's, and yet others, like Dolly, stayed there almost all their lives.

Below: The Works Outing - in this case an excursion undertaken by the employees of Hackett Brothers, of Halesowen, to Porthcawl. Dolly Allen is standing in the back row on the extreme right. Her earliest compositions were created to amuse work colleagues on social occasions. (All photographs in this section now in the collection of Ken Allen)

Above: Geoff Cartwright, and his drums, at St.Mary's Church Hall, Wednesbury, in the early 1950's.

The Best Years of Banding

Geoff Cartwright

I'm told that I first showed interest in drumming when I was about five, but I certainly can't remember ever wanting to do anything else. I was given my first small set of drums when I was about eleven. I think they cost my parents about twentyfive shillings. I progressed from there. They were not able to afford to send me to any lessons, so I taught myself, and later taught myself to read music.

I started playing with dance bands when I was fourteen. The first job I ever did was at West Bromwich Town Hall and I played with Frank Evans and His Orchestra from eight till twelve for a Fire Brigade Dance. Those were the days when dance bands were very smart - we were inspected to see that we were wearing black socks, and that our finger nails were clean! The band leaders wore tailed suits and we wore dinner suits. I didn't have one, but my Aunt, who was a teacher at All Saints School, took me to a tailor in Oak Lane, West Bromwich, opposite the bus garage, and Colin Herring made me a dress suit for £9.

It was a very formal dance. The ladies were escorted back to their seats, and had dance cards to be filled in. The gentlemen wore white gloves - it was quite an occasion, and for four hours work I was paid the princely sum of fifteen shillings, which seemed quite a lot to a fourteen-year-old. I remember the cabaret featured Rob Wilton, of "The Day War Broke Out" fame, and I met a double bass player called Bob Carter, with whom I became very good friends. Later on in

life he became the pianist with the Hedley Ward Trio, but at the time he was nick-named "Scatterbrain" - the title of a popular tune at the time.

After that I played with an accordian band led by Harry Bennington. The first job I did for them was at the Church of the Good Shepherd, West Bromwich. It was a wedding, and we hadn't long started to play when the two families got up and fought, and they laid them out on the stage.

I was always playing somewhere or other. For example, at the Elms Conservative Club they had a trio featuring Dicky Bolton on piano and Cyril Walker on alto sax. He was manager of Bert Shinton's cycle shop for years. One piece of luck I had was to come across a drummer who had just been sacked from the band playing at Tipton Baths. He was charged with finding his own replacement. He took me down to Tipton in his sports car and dropped me outside the baths. A chap came across the road from the Rose & Crown and asked me who I was? When I told him I was the replacement drummer he didn't look very pleased, but I followed him into the baths to find that he was the leader of the band!

So I found myself playing in Horace Randle's band. His father kept the Rose & Crown, and was also the local undertaker. Horace led the band and played the piano. The drummer had warned me that the only person that I would have heard of in the band was the second trumpet player - a chap named Jack Bradney. I was puzzled to find during the first half hour that we only had one trumpet player, and then, suddenly, a figure crossed the dance floor in motorcycle leathers and joined the band. The first trumpet player, Bert Toye, said to me, "That's Jack Bradney" - he's always noted for being late!"

During the interval Jack invited me for a drink of coffee and we had a good talk. He lived at Friar Park, where his father had a shoe-repair business. I told him I lived in Vicarage Road, and he offered me a lift home on his motorcycle combination. The drums had to brought home on the bus the next day! I played at Tipton Baths for some time, but at the end of the season I lost touch with the band.

One day I was in Wednesbury, and a car pulled up. It was an old Lanchester, and Jack Bradney rolled the window down to say, "Just the man I want! I 'm starting up a band on my own - are you interested?" We went to a house in Darlaston where a bass player named Harry Kearns lived with his mother and her twenty cats. Along with Jack Bradney, there was Bill Stevens, on trumpet, Hal Bromley on alto sax, Ray Britain from Bloxwich on tenor sax, Stan Tinkler on piano, Harry on bass and myself on drums. We had a few rehearsals - which were the only rehearsals we ever had - and then the work started to come in. At first we were known as Jack Bradney and the Hurricane Six.

Over the years we grew in size until we were three brass, three sax and three in the rhythm section, and a vocalist, and we played regularly every Monday and Saturday in the Conservative Hall, Wednesbury, as the Jack Bradney Orchestra. This continued for years and we acquired quite a reputation and a loyal following.

We did seasons at Bloxwich Baths for the manager, Big Bill Pickering, the Channel swimmer, and became very good friends with him. We also played at Walsall

Town Hall, and it was the time that big bands were beginning to go on tour. When they appeared at a local hall, they did not play all evening - a local band was expected to relieve them. For example, we were expected to relieve Bert Ambrose and His Orchestra and found ourselves playing at Bloxwich Baths and Walsall Town Hall that night. We had to hire a mini coach to ferry ourselves back and forth.

We were the first band to play in West Bromwich Baths, and did many seasons there. We played opposite a number of well-known bands, such as The Squadronaires, Maurice Winnick, Jack Payne etc. For a long time we ended up playing at Stourbridge Town Hall in the summer, and Stourbridge Baths in the winter. At one time I played seven nights a week. I even played on Sunday nights, at the Italian Club in Edgbaston. I played there in a trio led by a genuine Italian, Reno Uccellini, from Wolverhampton. On other nights I could play at Brierley Hill Town Hall, or join Jack Bradney at a little ballroom next to the Crown at Albrighton, called the Palace.

During the War I was called up, but after I had completed my battalion training I was transferred to a band (the Regimental Band of the 52nd LI, 2nd Battalion Ox and Bucks LI), even though I had to change regiment to do so. My marching experience with a side drum was useful, because when I left the Forces in 1946 I came back to West Bromwich and joined the Borough Band. We had to march the Mayor to church

and back during his annual parade, and also take part in Remembrance Sunday parades. In 1972 we won the BBC Midlands "Birmingham Brass" competition, and for years afterwards, we were runners-up.

After the War I also returned to Jack Bradney and played with many other bands. Just after the War the Clifton Cinemas did a series of concerts called "Sunday Night At Seven", and I played at Sedgley, Coseley and Stone Cross, and then a similar series was presented at the Odeons. One of the nicest places I played was Dudley Town Hall where I appeared with Styx Wilkinson, whose signature tune was "Memories of You".

I played some traditional jazz with Jimmy Shelley's band, and some modern jazz at a pub called The Mitre, in Wolverhampton. The group consisted of Ralph Davis on trumpet, Trevor Horton on alto and tenor sax, clarinet and flute, Smokey Woods on vibraphone and Archie Cotterill, a brilliant jazz pianist from Wolverhampton. I provided the rhythm section along with a bass player called Len Rubery.

One of the great satisfactions of band work was the characters that I used to meet. Len Rubery was such a character. We used to drive around in his Austin Ruby, with my drum kit in the back and his double bass on the roof. I think he had learned to drive in France, and rarely drove on the correct side of the road. Another great character was Jack Riskit who

Below: Jack Bradney and his band, at Tipton Baths, 1938. Left to right: Ray Britton, Harry Kearns from Darlaston, on bass, Hal Bromley from West Bromwich, on alto sax, Celia Hylton, vocalist, from Pleck, Geoff Cartwright on drums, Jack Bradney, trumpet and *bandleader, Stan Tinkler from Walsall, on the piano, and Bill Stevens from West Bromwich on trumpet. (Photos in this section all from Geoff Cartwright's collection)*

Left: A Sunday band-concert at the Theatre Royal, Bilston, 1949, featuring Horace Bounsell on alto sax, Roland Swift, from Darlaston, also on alto sax, and Jack Harrison, from Wednesbury on tenor sax. Like Geoff, these musicians worked in local industry during the day, and devoted the rest of their lives to musical entertainment. The concerts were put on by Jack Riskit, who ran Bilston's theatre for Cyril Joseph who also owned eight local cinemas. Jack retired in 1953, and the theatre closed four years later.

ran the Theatre Royal, Bilston, where we performed some Sunday concerts. It was so dusty backstage that no-one dared sneeze for fear of disturbing the lot, and the dressing rooms lacked doors, but it was worth all this to meet Jack.

Jack lived in a little house next to the Rialto cinema, Wednesbury, and had once been a slack-wire artist. After we had played at the Theatre Royal, he would book us again to appear three weeks later, under a different name. He used to say, "No-one will know until the curtain goes up!"

I've been semi-professional most of my life. In the old days I used to earn £2.10/- for a night's work, so I always had to have a full-time job as well. During the day I would do work like driving a crane in a foundry. Sometimes I have played until three o'clock in the morning and have had to go straight to work in my dinner suit, change, and carry on with my day-time job. That's what we used to do. And over the years I have played at all kinds of functions, Jewish Golden Weddings, Sikh Weddings and an occasional Ceildh, but what I really like is the music of the Big Band era.

Jack Bradney is now a greengrocer in Priory Road, Dudley, and I don't think I can persuade him to come out of musical retirement to put a band together one more time, but I've still got my drum kit upstairs and I still play when I can.

The photograph at the foot of the opposite page, and the two on this page, are the work of Bob Hosier, who gives an account of being photographer at the Hippodrome, Dudley. By coincidence, one of his photographs was used on page 22 of "Black Country Folk at Werk". Bob Hosier worked in the drop forging industry, and he took the picture of the Massey hammer at Vaughan Brothers of Willenhall, where he worked. A copy of the picture found its way to the author's collection. It's a small world...

Left: At the end of October 1947 Dudley Hippodrome celebrated its ninth birthday, having opened in December 1938. (The birthday had to be celebrated early each year to avoid clashing with the opening of the pantomime.) Bob's picture shows the finale, featuring Webster Booth and Anne Ziegler in the centre of the picture. To their left are the Ben Abdrahman Wazzan Troupe of acrobats. The star of the show was Jimmy James.

Right: The 1944 pantomime at Dudley Hippodrome was "Aladdin", where Bob Hosier discovered his friend Alec Pleon was playing Wishee Washee. This is one of Bob's striking pictures of Avril Angers in the part of Aladdin.

Below: The 1945 pantomime was "Babes in the Wood", and this is one of Bob's pictures that was put in the theatre's display cases. The babes are Brian Lindsay and Mareda Osborne. Denise Clifford can be seen as Robin Hood, and Diane Stuart is Maid Marion. The substance of the show was largely created during rehearsal by the man on the left: Billy Russell, in the role of Billy Tipton. Billy was born in 1893 and grew up in Dudley. At the age of ten he was selling programmes at Dudley's Empire in Hall Street, and later went on the stage as a comic "on behalf of the working classes". He could adapt his regional accent to wherever he was appearing, as well as exploit his own Black Country speech. He died in 1971.

The Hippodrome Photographer

Bob Hosier

I inherited my interest in photography from my Father, who had a quarter plate Kodak, and I used to watch him printing photographs. I purchased my first camera from a colleague while serving my apprenticeship at John Thompson's, which I started in 1931. The first photograph I had published was taken by sticking my camera on top of a chocolate machine in Rhyl and taking a view of the Pavilion at night. It appeared in a brochure for Rhyl, about 1935, but I never got paid for it.

I was really fascinated by 35mm cameras and the tremendous enlargements one could make from 35mm film. I wished for a Leica camera, but they were too expensive, so my first 35mm camera was a Retina. During the early days of the War, a friend of mine knew an Austrian refugee who had a Leica for sale, so I acquired that. A suitably challenging subject for the f2 lens of the Leica was the theatre.

I read the Amateur Photographer regularly and learned about the Camera Club, in London, which had a 35mm section which included some of the top thirtyfivers in the country. I joined and found that every month they went to the Windmill Theatre on a Sunday to take photographs at the dress rehearsal - forty of them sitting in the front two rows of the circle. I went along, and really got bitten by the bug - from then on my interests were photography and the theatre. Another member of the club was a stage comic named Alec Pleon, and one day when I was in London, I arranged to meet him at the Prince of Wales Theatre where he was appearing with Sid Field in "Strike a New Note".

While travelling through Dudley just before Christmas in 1944, I noticed that Alec was billed to play Wishy Washy in Alladin at the Dudley Hippodrome. Once again I made contact with him, and I spent a lot of time during the run of that show taking photographs at the Hippodrome. Normally people were not allowed to take photographs, but Bob and Maurice Kennedy, who owned and ran the Hippodrome, were very friendly and helpful to me. At the end of the show's run they said, "Alec is going, but you can keep on coming!"

From then on I did just as I liked anywhere in the theatre, particularly during variety shows, and could come and go in the auditorium and backstage as I pleased. The pantomimes ran for three months which really gave the photographer a chance to get cracking, and when "Babes in the Wood", starring Billy Russell and Fred Kitchen Jnr., was presented in 1945, I went to weeks of rehearsals taking photographs right up to the opening of the production. I spent Christmas Day producing prints taken during dress rehearsals, and my pictures were put on display in the showcases outside the theatre. I had made good friends with most of the company, and from then on I was "in" - as the theatre's official photographer.

My real work was still drop forging, but I was at the theatre three or four times a week, and most Sundays. It was great fun to be there, and a wonderful opportunity for a photographer, even if I was never paid for it. My pictures included rehearsals, the shows themselves, and the life of the theatre backstage. For example, I took many pictures in "The Glue Pot" - a bar under the stage used by the cast after the show. It earned this name because once you were in there you got stuck! I installed a photoflood in the middle of the bar in order to take my pictures.

As well as meeting the artistes, there were other people who became part of the theatre's life, and who might be found in The Glue Pot. These people ranged from the Chief Constable, who shared my interest in photography, to local tradesmen and businessmen. Access to this social scene was controlled in as much as a list was put up in the office by the stage door stating exactly who might be admitted. I was relieved to find that my name was on the list, and, of course, the people I met often led me to other photographic assignments. For example, Mr. Preedy asked me to produce a photograph of the contented smoker to form the frontispiece to his cigar catalogue. Percy Mead, the head brewer from Hansons' Brewery invited me to join the trips to the hop fields when members of the Midlands Branch of the Brewers Guild made their annual inspection of the hops and attended a dinner.

Bob and Maurice Kennedy continued to be kind and helpful to me. They devoted their lives to their theatre, and they also ran the Plaza cinema next door, the Plaza theatre in West Bromwich, and they had an interest in the Mirabelle Dance Hall at the foot of Castle Hill. The stage manager, a great East End character named Jack Benson, also included me in many aspects of the work of the theatre. From 1945 onwards I joined him on an annual trip to London to inspect the Pantomime sets. As the opening of the panto approached, Jack would always say, "We'll never get it on." But we knew very well that we would.

The pantomimes were presented by Sam Newsome from Coventry, and as well as presenting the shows at Dudley and Coventry, he also did them at Northampton and Derby. As the years went by I found myself travelling round photographing all these shows, meeting the same people again and again as I went from show to show. Many of them became great friends and I became quite familiar with the world of theatrical "digs". In Dudley the place for these digs seemed to be Buns Lane. In my occasional capacity as a chauffer, I met artistes at Dudley Port station, or took them into Birmingham for a train that ran to London at midnight. It was never listed in the timetables, and was therefore known as the "Ghost Train"!

The backstage mechanics of presenting a show were fascinating, and for the weekly shows, the "get in" and "get out" were fantastic operations. Every Friday night the agent from the railway used to come with his book in which he recorded every move that would have to be made to transport the show from one theatre to the next. He had to work out how many lorries would be required, and how many trucks the railway would have to provide. The scenery had to be "got out" very quickly after the last show on Saturday night, and it had to be at the next theatre on Monday morning without fail.

Another member of the staff was Jack White, the Front of House Manager. He was interested in cinephotography, ever since being a cinephotographer for the Royal Flying Corps in the First World War. He was also a keen member of the Circus Fans Association, and through him I also met many people from the circus world. Another of Jack's interests was fireworks - he was a pyrotechnician. One night he put magnesium candles along the top of the theatre parapet. I went up there to help him light them, and we lit up the place for miles around.

Among the staff and friends of the theatre, life was always made more interesting by playing practical jokes on one another. I remember the morning that Jack Benson was organising the "get in" for "The Desert Song". His wife rang from their home in the Broadway to say that a lorry had just pulled up outside with a load of sand and the driver was demanding to drop it off!

On another occasion we were putting on a show featuring Dante, the great illusionist. His act included the use of a number of ducks, and the ducks arrived a week in advance of the show. They had to be found "digs" in the swimming pool at the Ward Arms Hotel, while waiting for the "get in" on the following Monday. Jack Benson thought this provided an opportunity for a joke. On the Monday the ducks were rounded up and hidden away. A butcher named Bill Scholey, who was a regular in the Glue Pot, provided the required number of ducks' heads that were then strewn around the pool.When the Touring Stage Manager went to the Ward Arms all he could find were the ducks' heads. Although Dante was an expert at making ducks vanish, the Stage Manager was dismayed when they vanished at the wrong time!

Perhaps it was Jack's revenge on animal acts. Whenever animals appeared at the Hippodrome it provided the theatre with an accommodation problem, and Jack would be saying, "I can't bear it this week - the place will stink by Saturday." One tatty lion lived on the stage for a week, on the end of a chain. He was pretty sleepy and we often had trouble waking him to do the show.

My best photographic work covered the pantomimes, because that was when I had the best opportunities. People in Dudley used to complain about the Pantomime running for three months, while people came to the theatre from miles around, but they weren't very good at supporting it for the rest of the year. Of course there were fantastic sell-outs, like the two shows put on in one night by Bob Hope, but the variety shows couldn't always fill the theatre. When I look back on the ten years I was the theatre's photographer, I don't just think of the photographs and cine film that I took, I also think of the hundreds of interesting people that I met and the friends that I made.

Below: Bob Hosier's views of life backstage at the Hippodrome include this picture of scenery arriving on stage ready for the "build up".

Above: On 13 May 1990 Stourbridge Film Society organised a film show at the Danilo, now a Coral Bingo & Social Club, to mark the fiftieth anniversary of the cinema's opening. The Chief Operator on that day in 1940 was eighteen year old George Salt, seen here fifty years later, with his wife Betty, whom he met when she joined the staff as an usherette. On their left: Georgina Chatterton, ex usherette, and right: Joan Groves who was a cashier in the 1940's. In this section of the book four people give an account of working on the Danilo circuit. (Express & Star)

Putting on the show - at the Danilo

George and Betty Salt

George Salt: Mortimer Dent opened his first Danilo cinema at Brierley Hill in 1935. Two years later he opened the second in Redditch. I joined the staff at Redditch not long after it had opened. I was engaged as a trainee operator. (There was no Sunday opening at the time and the Danilo's programme could be presented with three operators.) The Chief was one of the "old school" and had been an operator all his life - when he trained you, you really felt you were being trained! I had to learn to keep the box spic and span - if there was a speck of dust anywhere you would soon know about it. I was not allowed to graduate to rewinding the films until I had learned to dust and polish.

As I moved on to rewinding I was shown how to examine the films, and how to make joins where the films had broken. In those days they were all nitrate films and we didn't use film-splicers. A joint was made by hand - held together between our fingers until the joint was effected. Then we had to put a "V" on the soundtrack with Movietone black ink to stop the "plop" as the joint went through the sound head of the projector. When safety film came out we had to learn to use the splicers.

I worked my way up to Second Operator, and in July 1939, Mr. Dent's secretary asked me if I would go over to the Danilo Brierley Hill as a "Relief" for a few days. I did not take much with me, and, of course, had to find temporary lodgings - but I stayed six weeks! Once Brierley Hill's problems were sorted out I returned to Redditch. However, in October, a month after the War had started, I was asked if I would return to Brierley Hill "just for a few days". I refused as I remembered how the days had become weeks last time. In the end Mr. Dent himself came to see me and said, "I'll tell you what I'll do - I'll make a bargain with you - if you go over to Brierley Hill, I will give you Stourbridge when it opens next April or May."

He was as good as his word. I transferred to the new Danilo at Stourbridge about a month before it opened - and found there were plenty of jobs to do in preparing the cinema for use. One of the first jobs that I did was to hang the "black-out" curtains. The holes I drilled to hang those curtains have not been filled - and can still be seen today! We experimented with the equipment and lined up the new projectors. These were the latest Ross GCs, not like the old ones I had worked with at Redditch and Brierley Hill. I was just eighteen years old, which was pretty young to be a "Chief", but they seemed satisfied with my work, and I never had any problems.

The cinema opened on 13th May 1940 with "At The Villa Rose". The War was on and the Bank Holiday had just been cancelled so we just opened in a rather subdued way at 2 o'clock on that Monday afternoon. There were no crowds or ceremony. I had a Second Operator and two trainees working with me. During 1940 we were not just showing pictures - we also had to do fire-watching at night.

I was living in lodgings in Worcester Street, and after the evening show I just had time to nip home for a bit of supper before returning to the Danilo. I locked myself in and made for the camp bed in the rest room. If it was a quiet night I could get my head down for a few hours, but even if it was not I still had to be at work at 10.30. the next morning. I remember the night Coventry was bombed. I had never seen such a marvellous sight - the flares were beautiful colours, but, of course, it was also frightening.

The money in the cinema business was terrible but it was something I wanted to do, and it's a trade that gets hold of one - it's very difficult to leave it. We were generally left alone to get on with our job. Even when Mr. Stanley, the circuit supervisor came round he rarely came up to the operating box. Only one manager ever gave us any bother, and that was Mr. Lingard. At the back of the stalls there was a button which he could press if he thought the sound was not adjusted correctly. He would press it once and we would turn the sound up, he would press it once again and we would turn it up further. Invariably he would then press the button twice which was the signal to turn the sound down, so we would return the volume to its original level. The buzzer would be going all night!

We had many jobs to do, and our day started at 10.30.am. We had to clean the arc lamps and check the machines. We had to clean and maintain the stage lighting, particularly the footlights. If the doorman was off I had to stoke the coke-fired boiler or clean the flues. Late at night after the show had finished we had to brave the cold to change the lettering that announced the programme on the cinema's canopy. On Sunday mornings I often had to go in to make up the programmes if the films had arrived late. We were allowed one day off per week, but never at the weekend, and one early finish at about five o'clock. If the men came in at night to respray the screen I often had to stay there all night, and was allowed half an hour off the following morning!

Because the pay was so bad and the hours so unsociable it beacame more and more difficult to keep staff. A youngster would come and be trained but would then leave to earn more money at the Kings or the Odeon. Sometimes I found myself working alone - doing all the change-overs every twenty minutes, and dashing to rewind the film reel by reel. When S.M. Cinemas took over they gave us double pay during Christmas week, and double pay for our one week's annual holiday.

Eventually they decided to allow women to be operators, and they asked some of the usherettes if they would like to learn film projection. I trained quite a few of them and created a good team. Margaret Lowe trained to become Second Operator, and others included Margaret Cottren, Pam, Connie Rose etc. We were proud of our showmanship. We even took great care over the records we selected and played - and patrons would send an usherette up to the box to ask about the music. We used to open the main curtains about five minutes before the show and take control of the lights from the dimmer room, sliding the resistors up and down, playing the colours on the second curtains until the adverts started. And, of course, we used to spotlight the icecream girls in the intervals.

Patrons were keen to see the news, and sometimes we put on an extra showing of the news at the end of the evening's programme - British Movietone News at the time. Later we showed Paramount News , then Pathe. We shared Pathe news with the Savoy. Sometimes there was only five minutes between their showing and ours - and, on Saturdays, you couldn't get through the crowds in town from the Savoy to the Danilo in five minutes, even if you were running with the newsreel under your arm.

My service at the Danilo was interupted by being called up in 1942, but I was able to return in 1946. Mr. Dent sold out to Mr. Southan Morris, who was a very nice man, and later the cinema joined the Essoldo group, but up in the box we never heard about such matters until after they had happened! In 1954 I installed new wiring for Cinemascope and arranged the masking for our screen, but somehow I felt the end was coming. The Danilo had never managed to present as popular films as the Kings and the Odeon. The War had prevented Mr.Dent from expanding his circuit and we could never compete with the our bigger rivals. I left in 1955, and the Danilo survived for only another eight years. Of course I missed the cinema business. I have since spent thirty five years making plastic buckets in Cradley Heath, but I am glad to have been part of the entertainment business. Somehow we seemed to get to know all the stars - even if we couldn't speak to them.

Betty Salt:

During the War I worked in Kidderminster in a munitions factory, but after the War I became fed up with work in the factory, so I went for the job that came up at the Danilo. The night I started my cinema career George was standing in the foyer as I arrived. I thought he must be a relief manager so I said, "I'm the new usherette and I don't know where to go." Two nights later we started going out with one another. After I had been going out with him for a day or two I had to ask the Head Usherette what George's surname was because he hadn't told me! When we started courting we managed to make our days-off coincide.

I used to wear a green uniform, and the Head Usherette, Pat Hughes, inspected us and gave us our orders, although there was one manager who insisted on inspecting us! We would work one night downstairs and upstairs the next. If there were two of us on duty one would take the tickets while the other showed patrons to their seats, and, of course, we had to sell the ice cream. If it was packed, people had to stand at the back of the stalls, and they would argue over who was next in the queue as seats became available!

We got to know the regular patrons, but sometimes our audience was just the overflow - people who could not get in at the Kings or the Odeon. We knew the husbands and wives, and we knew the husbands with other mens' wives because such couples tended to come in separately and sit separately for a little while before moving to be next to each other. At the end of the evening the manager used to go mad if we didn't tip all the seats back. We then used to find all sorts of things that patrons had left behind - from half crowns to false teeth. Sometimes people used to kick their shoes off while watching the film and we would have to search for them, and sometimes patrons fell asleep during the show so we had to wake them up to send them home.

I loved working in the cinema but it was badly paid - I had to find myself a part time job in the morning, cleaning a woman's house, to make my money up! The strange thing is that I later went back to work part time at the Savoy. The pay was so low I must have been mad to go back. And it was so cold at the Savoy when the cinema was half empty that we had to stand by the radiators all the time.

I was at the Savoy when the decimalisation of money took place. Tim Williamson, the manager, organised training sessions to practice using the new money, but I was still fifty pence short after selling the ice creams on the first night. I had to make it up out of my own money.

If you work in a cinema you are usually given passes to other cinemas - so what did we do on our day off after working all those hours in the cinema? We usually went to the pictures.

Right: Derek Simmonds seen lacing up the projector at the Danilo, Stourbridge, where he was taught the skills of film-projection and presentation by George Salt. Derek, now the well-kown proprietor of Derann Film and Video Services in Dudley, found this picture in his own collection when the Danilo's 50th anniversary was being organised. His comments on it are reproduced here. (Royston Campbell)

Derek Simmonds

The photograph was taken during the screening of the Twentieth Century Fox Scope picture "Bus Stop", starring Marilyn Monroe. The Danilo put on a special promotion: a Marilyn Monroe "look-alike" contest on stage, and a bus driving round Stourbridge advertising the film. A photographer (Royston Campbell) came into the cinema to photograph every member of the staff carrying out his or her duties, from the doorman stoking the boiler, to the manager.

The photograph shows me lacing up the second reel of the film on our original Ross GC2 projectors. These were carbon arc machines, and we used to run on 40 amps in the afternoons, banging it up to about 50 amps in the evenings to penetrate the cigarette smoke! If it was foggy outside the air-conditioning system could drag some of the fog in - making the beam of light from the projector show up brilliantly.

I started at the Danilo, Stourbridge, when I was about fifteen and a half - trained by George Salt, who was a very strict Chief Operator, but a very good teacher, and 100% at his job. I went from trainee to fourth, to co-third, to third, and then moved to the Danilo, Quinton as second. Then, at eighteen, I had to go in the Army for two years. When I came back I returned to the Danilo, Stourbridge, to find that Cinemascope had been installed, so this picture was taken when I was twentyone.

(They had a special anniversary week at the Danilo when Cinemascope was five years old. We showed two scope features every day, changing the programme daily.)

I left the Danilo about 1958, because I felt it was about to close. No one would spend any money on it - we were taking lamps out of the house lights to conserve electricity, and the last straw for me came when we were forbidden to use the colour lighting on

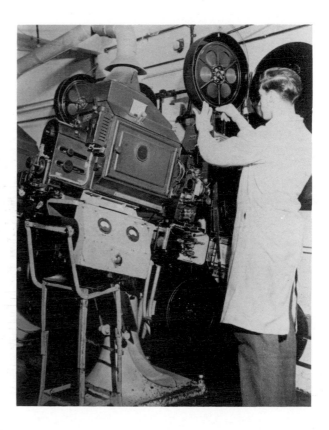

17

the stage. I didn't like that. I considered a job as a spot man at the Birmingham Hippodrome, but it wasn't practical to take it, although stage lighting had always been one of my major interests. I was offered the job of manager at the Royal, Cradley Heath, and I ended up working there part time while joining the Co-op as a baker - on a bread round.

A year or two later, while I was managing the Furniture Department of the Co-op store in Halesowen, sound films began to become available on 8mm. I bought a Eumig Mark S projector and a sound film. By the time I had a dozen films, it had occured to me that there would be demand for an 8mm Film Library - so I used those dozen films to start one. My son, Stephen, was born then so we used the £50 maternity benefit to start the business!

We ran the Film Library for many years, from a shop in Holly Hall for a time, and then from Dudley. We have moved into film distribution, hi-fi, video, video distribution and video production. And now we have started the film library again, and because there is no one else left to do it, we have to put the magnetic sound stripe onto the 8mm film ourselves - we will probably be the last people in the world to go on doing it!

I still have a soft spot for the Danilo - it was a lovely theatre. The Council missed a great opportunity of buying it and creating a theatre in the town with good satge facilities, just as Dudley missed the chance of saving the Hippodrome. What wonderful places they were.

Jan Bruton

I started work in the cinema business when I was about sixteen, by becoming an usherette at the Odeon. I worked my way through each department, and, one day, a vacancy occurred in the projection room, but it was Odeon policy not to allow females to train in that department. I knew I wanted to be an operator up there in the box surrounded by machines.

A few weeks later I ran into a friend of mine, Ron Homer, who was manager of the Danilo, Brierley Hill. (It had become the Essoldo, but we still thought of it as the Danilo.) He offered me a position as a trainee operator, and so I started at the Danilo as a No.7. They had three operators and five trainees at the time, and I was determined to work my way up to "Chief". It was Essoldo policy that a woman could not become Chief, so, technically Ron was Chief as wall as Manager, and my cousin, Marlene Holt was Second Operator. Essoldo policy changed and they decided a woman could be Chief provided she had done the additional electrical training. Josie Bray became our first woman chief while I was still five away from that position. I kept my sights fixed on my goal, but I little knew what the job entailed.

Looking back on it, there were lots of scary jobs to do, and I suppose they were anxious about women doing them. I had to content myself with starting as rewind girl, and I rewound many miles of film, but I always did it properly: I always washed my hands before rewinding and never let a scratch get on the film. I hated to see films that had been damaged by careless projectionists. There was quite a large turnover of staff at the time, and many trainees left because they did not like the unsocial hours. It was also a time of staff-cutting, so by the time I became Chief there was often only me and one trainee presenting the show!

I liked to perfect the timing in presenting a show. When we had Cinemascope films from Twentieth Century Fox, I used to practice the opening several times so that my timing was perfect. I could press one button to open the screen masking and the other to raise the festoon curtain just as the Twentieth Century Fox titles came on the screen. I was always upset if the opening title was mutilated. If it was I used to mount my push bike and go over to the Danilo Stourbridge to beg a good title sequence of Derek Simmonds, who was my opposite number in Stourbridge, and who kept his own little collection of such things! Then I would splice the borrowed piece of film onto our print! We would also swop gelatines for our footlights if we thought the lighting could be made more appropriate to a particular film.

I was forever complaining to Mr.Baker, the area engineer, that one of our curtain motors ran dangerously fast, but he wouldn't replace it. It gave us many headaches, and I've even had to stop a show to go down and sort things out. One day the screen masks opened perfectly but the festoon curtain stuck half way up, and would not budge. In the end I had patrons from the audience holding a steel cable wrapped round two rows of seats, steadying the cable as I climbed a ladder to the top of the screen. As I perched at the top of the screen I had to steady myself with one hand against the back wall, while I used the other, in which I held a screwdriver, and tried to disentangle the curtain cable from the corner of the screen. If anybody had sneezed I would have fallen to my death. One patron said, "Mate, I've worked on scaffolding,, but I wouldn't have your job for the world!" - but I had to do it because I was Chief.

I used to enjoy the morning work, particularly when I worked with cousin Marlene at the Danilo. We felt that presentation had to be matched by preparation - it was no good presenting a perfectly timed show if the lighting was dirty. We used to love to practice our timing, manually operating the gramophone, the house-light controls, the machines and the curtain motors, but the first thing we did each morning was the cleaning and preparation. We hoovered the stage and the curtains, brushed the screen, cleaned the gelatines in the footlights, and polished the reflectors.

In Brierley Hill it was not easy to keep a cinema clean. Many was the time we were rushing round the projection room profusely sweating but we dared not open the windows for fear of the smoke that would pour in from Round Oak Steel Works. If we did open the windows I would go home looking as if I'd climbed a chimney -there was that much smoke from the steel works.

One day we had a queue outside the cinema just as they opened one of the furnaces - filling the air with black powdery smoke. The wind blew it straight up the High Street. The buzzer went four times as the manager signalled to us that we should delay the start of the show. The patrons were crowded in the foyer and he was trying to dust them down. One woman's beautiful new coat was ruined. I can still remember

Ron shouting, "Don't start the show - I've got to dust the patrons!"

The cinema was a busy place under Ron's management. He ran a childrens' matinee club, and three football teams for the kids. He had a great sense of publicity. For example l remember the time when "Davy Crocket" was going to be screened. Ron went up to Brierley Hill Market and found someone in the rag trade who could supply us with three hundred Davy Crocket hats. Every kid in Brierley Hill wanted one of our Davy Crocket hats, everybody knew the film was coming, and it saved the firm a lot of money in advertising! He always had ideas like that for promoting the films, and that was why we could do better trade than the Odeon, even when they had better films.

One thing about working at the Danilo was that we never seemed to have time for proper meals. One day we spent the morning up at the Odeon, Dudley, for some reason, but on the way back Ron realised that we only had half an hour before our programme started. "Pop next door, Jan, and get a couple of cobs and a tin of soup," he said, "then dash upstairs, lace up the machines, carbon-up, and be ready for the show. By then I'll have the soup ready and the cobs cut."

I was just lacing up the second machine when the whole place shook. Our little kitchen was just below the box, and something must have happened to make the whole cinema rock. I raced downstairs to find Ron covered in tomato soup. Unfortunately, the cinema's white cat was sitting next to the gas ring where the can had burst. The next thing we knew was that an orange cat was running down Brierley Hill High Street - and we didn't see her again for six days. We never did eat anything that day. But we couldn't have

eaten anything anyway: we were laughing too much.

We guessed that the cinema would close long before it actually did so, and I left, about three years before closure, to go to work at the Royal, Cradley Heath. At the Royal I was still Chief, but I was usually on my own. That was brought home to me when Mrs. Dorsett, who ran the cinema, insisted on showing a film that had been banned everywhere else! Not only was I embarassed by the film, but I usually found I was the only woman on the premises. The equipment they used at the time was poor compared with the Danilo, but presenting a show on a shoestring was good experience for the final chapter in my cinema career.

I left the trade for a while and went into nursing. I eventually worked in the operating theatre where once again I enjoyed being surrounded by machines and equipment, but one day I met Tommy Watkins, who was an operator at the ABC Stourbridge. He put a good word in for me with the ABC's manager, Tim Williamson, and I was able to return to my work in the cinema. I retrained myself with the help of Tommy and Vic Court, who was about to retire from the business. Every cinema had different machines so there was always an element of retraining when you started at a new cinema, but at the ABC the machines even had different characteristics to each other!

I think the machines were made out of scrap pieces salvaged from other places. On arriving at work I would find a note from Tommy saying, "Middle sprocket is wearing - can you find a second-hand one from another cinema next time you're in Birmingham?" But it was great to be back in the projection room, working with machines again - but, it was not for long. On 6 November 1982 Tommy and I presented the last film, and the cinema closed.

Right: Jan Bruton, right, takes over from Vic Court, at his retirement from the ABC cinema, Stourbridge, in March 1982. Vic's fifty years as an operator had included work at the Temp and Clifton in the Lye, and the Kings, Stourbridge, before 28 years service at the ABC. Jan's return to the projection room was cut short when the ABC closed in November 1982. (County Express)

19

Always a Showman

Billie Kayes

Before I came to Great Bridge, I had been running the Amusements at a holiday camp at Morecambe, but on leaving there I was keen to find somewhere where we could settle down. Miles Jervis, the cinema proprietor at West Bromwich, was a personal friend of mine, and was helping us look for somewhere to set up in business. There was a vacant shop on the corner here in Great Bridge, and it seemed just the place to open a prize bingo. It was such a thriving little place at that time, with the big shops, and a good market place.

We didn't get the shop on the corner but we did get this one in Whitehall Road. We would have liked to be on the main street, but this was the only place available. We went out and put up bills and distributed leaflets announcing the opening of our prize bingo, and we started off very well. We stayed open until eight o'clock at night which was as late as our permit would allow, but business would have justified going on longer. Many years ago there had been an amusement arcade in Great Bridge, but prize bingo was new to the area. We had customers from Tipton, Dudley and West Bromwich, mainly people who had moved away from Great Bridge but still came back to do their shopping because they still liked the place.

In partnership with Miles Jervis we also opened a prize bingo in a new precinct at Kingstanding but that was later sold. I ran this business with Lydia Hickman, the widow of Charlie Hickman whose boxing booth was a well known feature of Pat Collins'

fairs in the Black Country and farther afield. A showman has to be fairly adaptable, and I already had experience of running bingo on the fairground - we used to call it Housy Housy.

At first I was always the caller, and there is a bit of an art in it. You have to know when to speed up, and when to slow down, when to talk, and when to get on with the game. In this type of bingo it's the number of games you can get through that counts, and the customers don't like waiting about. But the real essence of being a showman is the travelling, and that's what you miss when you settle down. I still have ties with travelling, and I'm still a member of the Showmen's Guild, but I don't suppose I will ever travel again now. I became a member of the Guild on 5th June 1939, my twentyfirst birthday, in our own circus tent on the fairground owned by Pat Collins at Aston.

We used to come to Great Bridge with Pat Collins' Fair, just down the road from here towards Greets Green. The ground was very soft and once the wind blew us down - it blew the front down and the tent's stakes wouldn't hold! Our circus toured with Pat Collins just before the War, and for a year or two after it. During our first season in the Midlands we had joined Pat Collins at just one or two of his fairs, Pat and my father liked one another, and Pat promised that he would try and find space for us if we joined his circuit the following year.

My family ran a circus, and a circus tent is a very awkward thing to fit into a fairgound. It can't go in the middle because that's where the riding machines belong, and it doesn't really fit on the sides. Our frontage was about thirty five feet long, but the tent we had then was about seventy feet diameter, creating gaps on either side of the frontage. However, Pat stuck to his promise, and if on some occasions there was no room for us we would go tenting on our own.

If we were tenting by ourselves, we would put on an hour and a quarter show, but on the fairground this had to be reduced to about half an hour, depending on how many people were coming at us, less if it was really crowded. We could pack about five hundred people into our tent, charging them 2d or 4d, or even 6d, if it was a good place. The wakes were cracking good fairs, and we visited many of them in the Black Country, sometimes doing a dozen performances a day. We came to West Bromwich, sometimes twice a year, to Wednesbury, Tipton, Darlaston, Blackheath, Wolverhampton and Walsall. We only ever went to Dudley once as it was such a small and awkward fairground, in Trindle Road. The biggest local fair was at Aston, where there were many shows, and Tom Norman and my father would try and out-parade one another in persuading the customers to see our shows.

Left: Wander off Great Bridge High Street into Billy Kayes' Bingo Parlour, and behind the microphone, by the "blower" that makes the random selection of numbers, you will find Billy himself. On the shelf above this machine is a photograph of Billy's mother, Rose, in a cage with a lion. The Black Country is always full of surprises like this: the story of the man from the circus who settled in Great Bridge. Bingo enthusiasts will note that the "blower" is a survivor from the pre-electronic era. It was built by Jim Pounder, a showman from the North East, and once provided numbers for bingo on the fairground.

My father, Richard Kayes, was in charge, and performed the horses as well as clowning. My sister Nora, who married Pat Collins' grandson, performed the trapeze, and I rode. My mother, Rose, also helped present the show, and, of course, we had to introduce other acts to keep the customers coming back. My family goes back a long way in show business. Grandfather Kayes was known as "Buff Bill", and he looked just like Buffalo Bill. He had seven children, including my father, and then after my Grandmother died, he married again and produced eight more children, including Tommy Kayes who used to perform the fastest lion act in the world on stage.

At one time my father ran a circus with his two brothers, and Uncle Timothy presented a lion act based on that of Tommy Kayes. My mother came from the Sedgewick family and had travelled with the menagerie, so really we were immersed in these show business traditions. We had always done other things as well, for example my father had run sideshows, and even Housy Housy many years ago. He spent a couple of summers at Sheerness with a slip and a set of gallopers, but he didn't like being settled down.

When the War broke out we were at Nuneaton. Everybody packed up, and we returned to the yard at Brownhills that we used for wintering while we were with Pat. We took the bodies off our lorries and converted them for carrying concrete air raid shelters for a contract. Then I was called up and went into the RAF. While I was in the RAF, they found I had a spot on my lung, and one lung had to be collapsed. That really put the kybosh on returning to the circus business.

After the War I did run the show for a short while, but it was too much for me, so I went into sideshows. In the end the circus had to be sold; the four horses, the lorries, and the tent. I bought a diesel-engined bus to travel with my sideshows. The fair doesn't seem the same now, but that's because it tries to appeal to teenagers. In my day we entertained the whole family, and our shows, and the sidestuff, were the backbone of the fair. Now it is the big riding machines that make the money.

I've been settled for nearly twenty years now, and unfortunately Great Bridge has declined in that time. The big shops have gone, and the place is nothing like it used to be. We still have a few diehards who were born and bred around here, but now other bingos have sprung up all around. We have had some really good regular customers, but of course some of them have died. They weren't young when we started, and young people are not bingo-minded. I enjoy being among people. I am very friendly with the customers, and they tell me their troubles.

Black Country folk are good spenders. If they've got money they'll spend it, but they are not awful moaners if they haven't got money. They are real good down to earth people, and I have enjoyed working here. It is a bit of a struggle now, and, because of my health, every day is harder, but I'll keep it going as long as I can. I will retire eventually I suppose, but real showmen don't like retirement. Having spent all these years giving out prizes, perhaps I'll win the pools.

Below: When War began in September 1939 Kayes' Circus was with Pat Collins' Fair at Nuneaton, but then packed up and returned to the winter quarters at Brownhills. For a few days "entertainment" ceased to exist: cinemas, theatres, and fairs were closed. Cinemas and theatres soon re-opened, and the fair found a way of concealing itself beneath "blackout". By Christmas 1939 Billy Kayes was part of the Roberto Brothers, appearing on horseback with Chapman's Royal Bengal Circus. Chapman's show opened at the Theatre Royal, West Bromwich on Boxing Day, and moved on later to Minehead. In the picture Billy is in the centre, with Roberto Germain (from Latvia) on the right. After leaving the show, Billy transported concrete air-raid shelters on the ex-circus lorries until he joined the RAF. (Nora Collins' Collection)

The chapter on the Emergency services begins with George Reohorn's account of his career in the Fire Service. It might be thought that photographs of large assembled throngs of workers like this one turn every individual concerned into one more anonymous member of the crowd, but when this picture was published in the Black Country Bugle a few years ago readers quickly responded with identification of those they recognised and remembered. Several readers recognised George Reohorn who is sitting on the front row seventh from the left! The picture was taken outside Wednesbury Fire Station in the early days of the War. George had graduated from being a "retained fireman" to having a full-time job in the service, and was about to take the first step on the ladder of promotion. The service's ranks are swelled by male and female members of the AFS, and photographs such as this one were used to publicise the work of the Fire Service and AFS in a drive for more recruits.

Left: After the War a photographer stood on the same spot outside Wednesbury Fire Station one damp evening to create this rather atmospheric picture in which a Commer and Dennis appliance can be seen. (All Fire Service pictures in this section are from the collection of George Reohorn)

2

EMERGENCY SERVICES

When the Bells Went Down

George Reohorn

By the time I left school at the age of thirteen, on 5th January 1919, I had already been working part-time for Watkins' Confectionery shop in High Street, Wednesbury, and had been learning how to knead bread for 12/6 a week. Graduating to full time work, I found that my working week went on until 7.00.pm. on a Saturday night, after which I had to go down to a pub in Lower High Street, to collect my wages. The boss was running the pub while his son ran the shop.

Our next-door-neighbour's brother-in-law worked at the Staffordshire Nut and Bolt Company in Darlaston, and he told me he could get me a better job, where I could finish at twelve on Saturday. So I started work there, for thirty shillings a week, and I could make hot bolts by the time I was seventeen. I worked hard and I played hard, and I never saved a penny, and I thought I had a job for life! I was married at twenty three, and shortly after my first daughter, Brenda, was born, the Managing Director of the Nut and Bolt Co. retired and withdrew his money from the company. The place closed - and there were no golden handshakes!

I was out of work for about twelve months, when Guest Keen took the firm over, reopened it, and re-employed the previous workforce. Thus I was making bolts again, but it only lasted for about eighteen months. We were promised jobs at their main works, in Station Road, Darlaston, but it never came to pass. There followed a period of three or four years when I was out of work, or rather, in and out of work, doing all sorts of jobs. Once a job lasted for six months when my brother got me a job at the Old Park Works of Metropolitan Cammell. At other times I would cycle miles to join Pat Collins' Fair at Atherstone, or Lichfield Bower, or once as far away as Crewe. My father, Billy Reohorn, known as Lump Coal Billy, was a traction engine driver for Pat Collins, and I could find casual work on the fair.

Early in the thirties, I realised I needed something to occupy my mind, and I joined the St. Johns Ambulance Brigade, and became a fully qualified First Aider. It certainly helped fill my time, and I used to put my daughter on the table at home, and practice bandaging! Apart from that, I found myself attending parades, and doing duties at places like the Hippodrome, and Wednesbury's three cinemas.

I eventually obtained a job in the Council's Highways Department, concreting, tarmaccing etc, and found that some of the chaps working with me were Retained Firemen at Wednesbury Fire Station. They told the Second Officer about me and my First Aid qualifications and he came after me three times to try and persuade me to become a Retained Fireman. I was not very keen on the idea at first, but, in 1937, I joined them. The retaining fee was £3 per year, and we were paid every time we "turned out" - 2/6 for the first hour, and 1/6 every hour thereafter.

We had to have a big bell fitted on our landing, and when that bell went off, it threw you out of bed. I also had to attend Tuesday and Friday evenings at the Fire Station to practice the drills. Competitions were organised where we could display our skills, running a line of hose out from the pump while throwing the suction hose into a reservoir, and directing the jet of water at a target. In teams of four we also practiced dry drills and ladder drills. I became very keen on the competitions and travelled all over the place taking part in them.

The Brigade also took the Mayor to church on Mayoral Sunday and Remembrance Day, and other local brigade representatives were entertained at these events. The Chiefs from Tipton and Willenhall came along with a couple of their men, and we would have a slap-up dinner in the Anchor Hotel. They reciprocated, but on a more modest scale, when they took their Chairmen to Church, but I was usually invited along on such trips as I was six foot tall and the Chief thought tall firemen looked the smartest. We had ceremonial helmets, made of brass, with "WFB" on the front, not like the black helmets we usually wore, which seemed to be only made of compressed cardboard.

At Wednesbury we had twelve Retained Firemen, and a full-time staff of three - a Chief Officer, a Second Officer and a Third Officer who also doubled as an ambulance driver. The station, in High Bullen, housed one fire engine which was a pump/fire escape appliance and one ambulance. The Fire Brigade was run by the Borough Council.

With the outbreak of War in 1939, I became a full-time member of the Fire Service. Wednesbury opened three sub-stations, one at McDougall's factory down Mesty Croft, one at Elwell's, Wood Green, and one at W.P.Edmund's, Kings Hill. I was put in charge at McDougall's with the rank of "Patrol Officer". We were given an office on the first floor, and a little kitchen. We built some bunks, and organised ourselves to accomodate six men on days, and six on nights. I worked during the day through to nine o'clock at night. Sometimes I would be half way home on my bike when the siren would go, and I would have to turn round, knowing that I would be up all night. Several times I worked forty eight hours without a wink of sleep.

At the sub-station we had two towing vehicles and two trailer pumps. We had an old London taxi-cab which towed the large Coventry Climax pump, and a Studebaker, which cost the council £80, which towed the lighter pump. I aslo had about fifty part-timers in the A.F.S., arranged in rosters of about ten men per night on a rota. When it got a bit warm at Coventry and Birmingham, I was sending a crew out every

night, as well as dealing with local calls. We had a flat roof above the office, and we usually sent an observer up there during an air-raid. I went up there myself during one raid. The Germans were dropping flares and it was as bright as day. We saw a plane pass over us, and I shouted, "Down you go!" As I followed him down the ladder, it was rocked by an explosion. A private house had been hit by a bomb targetted at the Bescot Railway Yards.

I went to Coventry one night, and it was just chaos - just a matter of "Pick Your Own Fire!" I picked one at the Co-op stores, and we had to walk through burnt sugar and Oxo cubes. It was the same night that the Cathedral was almost completely destroyed. We learnt to deal with situations by picking it up as we went along - just doing what you could to the best of your ability. I had a soldier seconded to me who had been in France, but he returned from Coventry a bundle of nerves. He'd never seen anything like it - France wasn't a patch on what he endured in Coventry!

In 1939 we decided to hold a Children's party in the Fire Station, which meant putting the appliances outside and decorating the interior. While twenty five feet up a ladder, hanging up a streamer, I slipped and fell. I knew I hadn't broken anything, but they put me in the ambulance and took me to Hospital, where I spent Chistmas in bed. The real climax of the story came after Christmas when they sent me a bill for five shillings for taking me to hospital in the ambulance.

The most memorable saga concerning that time took place in May 1941. It all began while I was taking the pumps down Hydes Road to the river Tame for their routine weekly test. At such times we always had one of our four messenger boys left on duty at the sub-station. We had just started the pumps when the messenger lad arrived on his bike, with a message from H.Q. "Report to Darwall Street, Walsall, immediately" - and that was it.

I thought they had a big fire and wanted assistance so we "made up" and drove to Walsall as quickly as possible. When we arrived a number of pumps lining up. It wasn't a fire - it was a regional call - and pumps were coming in from Willenhall, Darlaston, Brownhills and so on; about a dozen pumps in all. We were inspected by the Chief Fire Officer of Walsall, and then we were all sent on our way, and nobody knew where we were going except the officer in front of the convoy. I was told to bring up the rear of the convoy in our taxi-cab and pump.

It was still a mystery when we stopped at a church hall somewhere. The WVRS were putting on sandwiches. After this the troops were told to sleep on the floor of the hall, and Norman Bird, the Officer in Charge of the Convoy, and myself tried to sleep on the stage. A policeman had called and told us to be on the move at 4.00. am with a police escort. After a sleepless night, we found that some of the vehicles wouldn't start. In fact the one from Rushall had to be towed to get it started. But eventually we were underway, and we were escorted to Exeter.

At the Fire Station in Exeter they provided us with a hot meal and gave us two hours off, before preparing to move on again. Meanwhile we were joined by a convoy from Birmingham. In charge was a Brummie wearing brass epaulettes, and with too much to say for himself. I finished up as rear guard once more, and found out that we were bound for Plymouth.

On the outskirts of Exeter our towing attachment broke. We had a military escort - a motor cyclist at the front and rear of the convoy, so I told our despatch rider to go back and find some nuts and bolts to make a repair. When he returned I sent him on his way - after the convoy, leaving us to make the repair and find our own way onwards. How we found our way, I don't know, because all the signposts had been blacked out.

At the top of a hill we pulled up with steam pouring out of the radiator. The driver announced that the rad was bust, but I said, "Look we've come this far. If we have to bloody push it, we'll push it to Plymouth!" At the second garage we tried we were able to obtain some "Stop-Leak", but there we encountered a large lorry. The driver said, "Where are you bound for?" "Plymouth," I said.
"God help you! You won't come out alive you know!"

Right: The Fire Service and local factory fire fighting teams sometimes met for practices and exercises, as in this scene in the Tame valley by Bescot Marshalling Yard. In the foreground is a Commer vehicle, behind which, in the middle of the picture is an Albion that Rubery Owen acquired from Bridgnorth Brigade. On the right is a Fordson and behind that is another Albion.

"Thanks very much," I said, but I was pleased the crew had not heard his remark. While the man from the garage was attending to our radiator he sent us into his bungalow, instructing his wife to make all five of us a cup of tea, and give us some cake. We carried a square biscuit tin of "Iron Rations" on the appliance, so I gave her a quarter of tea from our rations for being so kind to us.

Ten miles from Plymouth we encountered the pump from Darlaston. It had broken down, and on the side was chalked, "I can hop it". We passed four or five other members of our convoy that had broken down, and then, on the outskirts of Plymouth we saw the "Billy Preston" - a large red van from HQ (Wednesbury Fire Station). The crew were in a cafe, so we turfed them out, but they were not very keen to proceed. It was growing dark, and people were pouring out of Plymouth in their thousands. After a cup of tea together we climbed back into our vehicles and the two Wednesbury appliances made their way into the city.

After reporting our arrival we were sent to a school building to rest. The roof was off the building, and we just lay down in our fire-fighting kit, as we had no blankets, and no other clothing. Other crews arrived all night, and some were sent to deal with a fire in the oil tanks at Devonport. Next morning we were sent to Stonehouse Docks, where a sub-station had been established. Some huge rolls of printing paper were on fire in a warehouse and we had to deal with it. We dropped our suction house into the water of the dock, and tried to get to the seat of the fire. Marines

were sent in to help move the paper, and delayed action bombs were going off all over the place. We eventually put the fire out, went back to the sub-station, and then across the road to the pub. We hadn't got a penny on us, as we had left Wednesbury at a second's notice.

The ten of us slept at the sub-station, and the next day I went to the Police Station to try and obtain a sub. It took a lot of doing, but I was eventually given £10, so that we could have £1 each. That night we went to the pub again, and once more we were all broke! I couldn't get a phone message home - that was out of the question. One of the crew wrote a letter to his wife, but I don't know if she ever received it. Day after day they said, "You'll be going home, tomorrow!" but, in the end, we were there for seven days.

We heard that a convoy, with a canteen van, was to assemble for a return to Walsall, but when we arrived it had already gone. There were the two vehicles from Wednesbury, and we found the pumps and crews from Willenhall and Rushall, so we made our own convoy, and away we went.

In the evening we stopped at a pub in Churchill, and the landlord was in the A.F.S.. He said we could sleep there, and led the leading fireman and myself down to the cellar, and we spent the whole night drinking. The next morning we set off, only to pause at Shepton Mallet, where the local Fire Chief again took us off for a drink! We arrived back in Wednesbury one afternoon. The Chief Officer immediately told me off because I had left the station without leaving anyone in charge. When I arrived home, I found no one was in. My wife had gone to her mother's, as she had not heard a word from me for over a week! And when I saw my daughter again, Brenda said, "Who's that man with a beard?" A week later the council stopped a pound out of my four pound wages to pay for the sub I had received in Plymouth.

Eventually the sub-stations were closed down, and I operated from the main Fire Station in High Bullen, and was promoted to the rank of Section Officer. Then I transferred to Darlaston, where I was second in command, and eighteen months later I went to Willenhall. We were all part of the National Fire Service by then, and the identity of the small local brigades was lost. In Willenahll I worked twenty four hour shifts, and we had some very happy times.

I remember VE Night in Willenhall. We were in the Red Lion, and the landlord was drunk. He told everybody to "pull their own", and everybody was happy. Then we were called out to Short Heath. We found the residents had built a bonfire in the middle of the road. They had used old tyres and all kinds of rubbish, and the local Bobby wanted this fire put out. We went to work, but the local residents, mainly women and children, set about us. The women called me every name under the sun, and the kids started banging the side of the appliance with bin lids. We

Below: On page 22 we glimpsed members of the AFS working alongside the Fire Service. During the War many Black Country folk worked in some kind of emergency service outside their "normal" working hours. Here we see Wednesbury Council workers who formed an ARP team led by Ray Vaughan, a foreman in the Council's maintenance department. Ray's team would disappear for days after the bombing of Birmingham and Coventry on ARP missions - rescuing people trapped in bombed buildings etc. (Edna Vaughan collection)

put the fire out, and decided we should leave as fast as we could, but the appliance wouldn't start. The driver had to wind it. The engine leapt into life, and, as we pulled away, the Bobby jumped on the back of the engine - he wasn't stopping there! Half way up the road we met the Senior Fire Officer on his way to the scene. I said to him, "Don't go up there, if you value your life!" It was dangerous to stop people having their fun on that night.

Shortly after the War I was promoted to the rank of Sub Officer, and returned to Wednesbury, and then became Station Officer, and reigned for sixteen years. First we lived at the back of the station, and then in the Station House, facing the main road. My family's life centred around the life of the Fire Station. For example, my wife used to cook dinner for the crew on duty. Times had changed and we had full-timers manning one appliance, and a second appliance manned by Retained Firemen. Once I would never have guessed that I could have led other men, or deal with the kind of situations that we encountered, but the Fire Service became my life.

One was supposed to retire from operational work at 55, but I managed to keep going until I was 57. I was then summoned to the Staffordshire HQ at Stone where they implied that I would have to go. I told them that I had more energy in my little finger than they could find in some of their chaps. I felt very angry about being forced to retire, but I couldn't fight it. At least I enjoyed five retirement parties!

I never regretted being in the Fire service, but I don't think we were well treated. I enjoyed the work, and always took a pride in how quickly my crew could "turn out". One night my crew was timed from the moment the bells went down to the moment the appliance began to move. It took us nine seconds.

Earning Your Corn

Joe Davies

Members of my family had been policemen in Shropshire, and there was a feeling in my family that I should join the police or work towards running a haulage business. When I left school at fourteen, a few years before the War, I joined a haulage business that had more horse and carts than motor vehicles. so I began my working life by driving a horse and cart, but I progressed to the motor side of the business in 1939. I stayed with them until 1941, when I joined the Army, and went into the Royal Army Service Corps.

I was involved with heavy haulage in the army, but my family were still trying to convince me that I should consider joining the police. It was possible during War Service to apply to a force, have the medical and take examinations so that you were prepared to join a force as soon as you left the Army. The Chief Constable in Wolverhampton was a very forward thinking man, well ahead of his time, and he was recruiting while the War was on. It also worked in our favour because, if accepted by a force, we were released from the Services early, following the cessation of hostilities. I came out of the Army in 1946, and went straight into Wolverhampton Borough Police.

I was kitted out in the cells, under Red Lion Street Police Station by a man named Ike Howell, who was P.C.1. In his time he had been a boxer, but by then he had become the gaoler, taking prisoners to court, and from court to prison. In his spare moments he looked after the stores. He was a hard man, and an excellent storeman, because he believed stock should stay on the shelves rather than be issued - saving the ratepayers' money.

I was sent for thirteen weeks training at Ryton on Dunsmore and started on nights the Monday night after I returned. Recruits were allocated to Red Lion Street or to one of the two sub-stations: one at Bushbury Lane, the other at Heath Town. I was allocated to Red Lion Street, and looked forward to about six weeks of nights while I was shown round the division.

The shift began with a parade, and we stood to attention as the Sergeant came down the passage shouting "Produce Appointments." We stood with our truncheons in one hand, and the handcuffs in the other, he looked round, and then shouted, "Return Appointments." That was the signal for the Inspector to appear from the passage. He read out our duties and the occurences of the last twenty four hours. Every man was also given a "Special Attention Card" relevant to his beat.

As a new recruit I was directed to join a senior constable, and then we were marched out of the station by the Sergeant, and up Darlington Street to Queens Square. Men dropped off to proceed to their beats, so it was essential that we marched in the correct order, with the man on the Chapel Ash beat at the rear. Men on town centre beats walked to them, but men proceeding to Penn or Finchfield took a bicycle and signed it out for the tour of duty. Men on the previous shift had to wait to be relieved - the beat never went unguarded.

Above: Joe Davies, PC 39 of Wolverhampton Borough Police Force, stands beside a "Star" car - built in Wolverhampton. Readers who like detective work are invited to date the picture.

Once on the beat, there were regular visits from the Sergeants, and at eleven o'clock you could set your watch by the regular appearance of the Inspector walking up Darlington Street with his big stick. He had a regular routine, visiting all the town centre beats, and you had to be there to see him pass your beat.

We had no radios in those days, and we relied on communication via the police pillar system. These were blue pillars with a lamp on top. If the light was flashing you were required to answer the phone in the box attached to one side of the pillar. If you failed to answer within ten minutes they would want to know what you were doing, so, no matter how you walked your beat, you had to make sure you saw one of these pillars at regular intervals. There were very few police cars - perhaps just one per shift, and not fitted with radios. The pillar also supported a box that could be opened by the public containing a mouthpiece that connected them to the station.

Once you had been shown round all the beats, you went through the traumatic experience of be turned loose on a beat all on your own. It would seem a very long night, broken by only a half hour break in the station for drinking coffee from an enamel mug. The beats were carefully allocated so that a senior constable was always on the adjacent beat to a new man, and as a junior you always started on a beat like Chapel Ash which was quieter than the town centre itself.

There were so few cars about then that if you saw a car on your beat, you were expected to know what it was doing. Parked cars were supposed to have parking lights - which was a marvellous thing for the police because it meant that no-one dared park all night for fear of flattening their battery. There were still military camps around Wolverhampton. and vehicles were often stolen for a joy ride back to camp, so it was a good idea to check all vehicles.

The Inspector responsible for allocations watched our progress carefully, and moved us towards the town centre if he felt we could look after ourselves. Although I was young, I was fit, reasonably well built, and could look after myself, so I made good progress towards the town centre beats. Wolverhampton was a rough town. Many men were returning from the Services. They had a lot of money and were blowing it, and were giving the town centre a hard time. Drunkeness and fighting were common problems. Some people think we have problems now - well, we certainly had problems then, just after the War. A night on the beat was very exciting!

Dudley Street and Stafford Street were the worst spots, and one night I had taken over Dudley Street while the older man checked the property on his beat. The licensee of The Shakespeare in Queens Square came rushing out. It was being smashed up. I went in through the front door to find it was a shambles. Chairs and tables were smashed, and a locally notorious family had started the trouble. They had escaped through the back into Woolpack Alley. I tried to head them off, and as I entered Queens Square, a large shop window went. The three men I was chasing were heading out of the square towards the Lytch Gates.

I caught up with them, and challenged them, and quite a fight developed. I was very fortunate in that I was able to lay the three of them out on the floor. The night shift came parading up Darlington Street at just the right moment, and I think some of the senior men were quite impressed to see the three men laid out - I had justified my existence in the town centre.

Hauling struggling prisoners from Dudley Street to Red Lion Street was quite an exhausting problem. If you were very lucky there might be a driver available who could bring the prison van, and, of course, you could only summon help with the whistle, or by using the police pillars. Self preservatiuon taught us to be tactful, and not to wade into situations we couldn't handle.

In those days there were constables who spent their entire thirty years service on the beat, so I was very lucky to have an opportunity to move on. I had worked the streets for two years when, in 1948, I heard there was talk of starting area cars equipped with radio. Inspector Llewellyn was building up this side of things, and he had to find out who could drive, and select six men from the force who could be sent away for training as police drivers. I had been driving since 1939, and was lucky to be selected and sent to Preston for the course.

I went out on the first night that area cars with radio were sent out in Wolverhampton, and, again I had a bit of luck. I made the first arrest in Wolverhampton that was made as a result of radio. Each car had a driver and an observer, and we were sitting in our Wolsley 18 when we received a message saying that a lorry had been stolen at Fordhouses. We spotted it in Stafford Road and gave chase. The driver dumped it in Renton Road and escaped, but we tracked him down and made an arrest. That gave me another good start.

You were only seconded to the cars for a month, and if Inspector Llewellyn felt you were not pulling your weight he would put you back on the streets the following months. It became my ambition to be permanently allocated to the Traffic Department. Life had to be totally dedicated to the task, and I carried a portable typewriter with me in the car so that I could write up my paper work immediately after an incident. Reports went to the Superintendent at 9 o'clock and the offender usually appeared in court that day. Many a night shift was followed by a day in court. And the next night we had to be on duty again with the car spotless brecause the Inspector was as proud of his vehicles as he was of the efficiency of his men. He really made us earn our corn.

I fulfilled my ambition of joining the permanent Traffic Department, and sometimes at night I was the only "mobile" person on the force so I really felt I was on the frontline. It was hectic but I enjoyed six years of that work. Then I passed my sergeant's exams, and, in 1954, became the first post-War recruit to become a sergeant - and thus I found myself back on the town centre streets!

Although I had a successful career in the police, it mustn't be thought that I was never in trouble. While I was still a fairly junior constable I was showing a new recruit around one night, in the Richmond Road area - out in the sticks. We were both on cycles, and in York Avenue a hedgehog crossed the road in front of us. I said to Tommy, "Look at that bloody thing!" We went off duty at six, but I was woken at ten and was told that the Superintendent wanted to see me. I dressed in uniform and reported to Superintendent Pendered - an ex-Guardsman who, as Deputy Chief Constable, was responsible for discipline. He was a real Wolverhampton man and very down to earth.

"Davies, where was yo' at 3 o'clock this morning?" he asked as he glared at me.
"I'll have to look in my book, Sir," I replied.
"Yo' doh need to look in that bloody book. I kno where yo' was. Yo' was up York Avenue, and we have received a very serious complaint from a lady. She was looking out of her bedroom window at 3.am. and yo' was heard to say, 'Look at that bloody thing!'"
"Oh," I said, "I never saw that lady at all. All I saw was a hedgehog crossing the road, and that's when I used that expression."
He hit the table so hard, I thought he was going to smash it. He thought he had got me. "How the hell did yo' think that one up so quick?"
I insisted that he could check my story with Tommy, and very reluctantly he was cooling down as he was almost tempted to believe me. Even so, he had to have the last word:
"Davies, if yo' want to cuss in the streets, go up to the top - into the bloody fields, where they can't hear yo'."

Fetch the Midwife!

Winnie Large

Although I was born in Birmingham, on 27th October 1899, I grew up in Newcastle Under Lyme, in a family consisting of four sisters and one brother. When my eldest sister and myself left school we had to do the domestic work in our house. My mother had always had help, because she was not domesticated, but we were taught how to do the domestic chores, and we dispensed with Lucy, who had done all the work for years.

From the day I left school I had always gone to Night School and had become a member of the St. John's Ambulance Brigade, but I first encountered the world of nursing as a patient. I developed a serious hip condition and had to spend a long time in the North Staffordshire Royal Hospital. I was there for so long that I became attached to hospital routine. From there I was sent to a sanitorium to recuperate.

When I was better, I joined the domestic staff, I did not know what else to do because there was nothing else I had learned. I became the Matron's maid, and found that it was a very nice job. All I had to do was take her meals to her, and keep her two rooms tidy, and I did that for two or three years. She was a very nice person, but she was fairly old, and therefore she decided to retire. Her staff were all very attached to one another, and very loyal to her, so they all decided to resign at the same time - and I went along with them.

I applied to train as a nurse, but never believed that they would accept me because of my hip operation. I went through a strict medical examination in which they looked at my heart and lungs in case of any chest complaint, and they looked at my legs and feet, in case I had varicose veins or flat feet. I passed everything, but they never asked me about surgery so I told them nothing. About two years later they found out because I had another illness and the doctor saw the scars. The Matron was furious, but it was too late.

I trained at the City General, Stoke-on-Trent, and it was a very good training school. It was very strict, but we had some good fun. State Registration was coming into force just as I started my nursing career, so I was one of the first State Registered Nurses. I had passed my exams at the end of the first eighteen months, and at the end of three years, so they offered me a job as a staff nurse.

It wasn't long before I saw a vacancy advertised for a post as Sister, and that's how I came to New Cross Hospital, situated between Wolverhampton and Wednesfield. I became a Sister on the Children's Ward, to which they added a Maternity Ward, and a Sun Ray Ward - they kept me very busy!

Winne Large and the brass plaque once attatched to the front of her home in Wednesfield. It was very important to make it clear that Winnie was properly qualified "by exam" in persuading people to use trained midwives. For a time an ante-natal "clinic" was held in her front room and her husband, a qualified male nurse had to test urine samples in the bathroom.

The Grand Theatre used to send six tickets for a Monday night show to the staff of the Work House, and six to the staff at New Cross Hospital. The Matron used to give these out, and one night I was given a ticket. Tom Large, who had started in the hospital as a Casualty Attendent, was also there, and bought me an icecream during the interval - and that's how I met the Wednesfield lad who became my husband. He studied nursing and became a State Certified Male Nurse - the first male nurse at New Cross, and he spent all his working life at the Hospital.

We were married in 1931, and in those days I had to leave nursing as soon as I was married. That's when I decided to go into District Midwifery on my own. We lived with Tom's mother for eighteen months while the houses were being built in Woden Avenue, but then we were able to move into a home of our own and I was able to put up a brass plaque stating, 'W.C. Large - State Certified Midwife - by exam.' I've still got the plate today, and at the time it was vey important to establish one's qualifications because then any woman could claim to be a midwife, and could do so legally as long as she notified the patients' doctors of the births.

Until I arrived there had never been a qualified midwife in Wednesfield, and naturally people were keen to turn to someone who did have proper qualifications. The local handywomen who had attended deliveries up until then resented my arrival at first, but they were fairly elderly, and retired from the scene. I was setting up on my own and therefore I had to charge my patients, although I varied my charge according to their financial circumstances. I had a friend, with whom I had trained, and she had set herself up as District Midwife in All Saints Road, Wolverhampton, so she was able to give me all sorts of help and advice, and she told me what I should charge.

Generally I charged twenty five shillings, and for that the mother would be on my books from the fourth month until the baby was a month old. I would be responsible for mother and baby for all that time. Some people could only afford to pay me sixpence a week - they had their children on the 'never never,' and sometimes they were still paying for the first by the time the second had arrived. But if people did owe me money, I forgave them if they were having difficulties. Some people obtained maternity benefit from their insurance policies, and I would only be paid once the insurance man had called. Good payers used to warn me, 'I see you've got Mrs --- on your books. Watch out - her insurance man comes on a Saturday. Be there when he comes if you want your money!' I'm sure I'm still owed some money today, but I don't think I'll ever get it now.

In a way I did too well, I got so much work, it nearly killed me. I don't know how many babies I delivered over the years, but there were one hundred pages in each register, and each page held ten cases. I filled eleven books over the years, kept them all for a long while, and then made a bonfire of them, I had a phone fitted at my own expense, the first in Woden Avenue, and, of course, the calls invariably came at night. One year I delivered three babies on Christmas Day. I had only one maternal death in all those years, and on that occasion Dr.Bentley, the Medical Officer of Health was present. The mother just gave a gasp in the middle of a contraction, just as the baby was about to be born, and she had gone. She seemed a healthy woman, but I had asked the doctor to be present because I knew her mother had died in childbirth. I asked the doctor if I could get the baby out, but he said, 'No - leave the poor little bugger there - its got no mother.' So that was that.

There were some large families in Wednesfield, and one lady, in Wood End, produced twenty three children, but only about thirteen of them lived. She had twins twice, but otherwise had one a year. She was "happy go lucky" and got by all right with a little help. Dr. Bentley used to send her a joint or a turkey at Christmas. She was also a very clean and houseproud woman, she even used to polish the waste pipe from her sink to the drain! I saw some very poor people, some filthy creatures, and also posh ladies and doctor's wives. Generally people had deliveries at home because it was cheaper than going to New Cross and paying three guineas a week.

Eventually midwives ceased to work for themselves, and were taken into the system. Ironically I earned far less when I was given a wage, than I would have earned if everybody had paid me when it was private. And there were a lot of rules to keep and a lot of writing to do. I had to notify the Medical Officer in Stafford within twenty four hours of every birth, and also had to state whether a doctor had been called, and if so, for what reason. The county had a supervisor who came round unexpectedly to try and catch you on the hop.

I loved my work, I liked the companionship with my patients, and my patients liked me. We didn't have many quarrels - except when the child was the wrong sex, as if it was my fault! I did occasionally tell the men off when they were producing children every year, and they couldn't afford it, but generally I got on well with everybody. Mind you, the men were rarely around at the birth. They usually went for a drink. Even doctors didn't really like to be present, they were always "too busy". Dr.Bentley made sure he never arrived until it was all over, unless it was an emergency. Dr.Bentley was a Wednesfield man, his father was the policeman, and he was a good doctor who practically worked for nothing! He'd say, "I ain't bloody well coming - she never pays." And then, at the next minute he'd be at the door because he was a man with a conscience and a heart of gold.

During the War, the women of Wednesfield had a hard time with the men away. I found myself running first aid classes on Monday evenings at Wood End School - teaching adults how to deal with air raid casualties. I enjoyed doing that. I was a casualty myself once. I was cycling along one day with Jerry flying overhead when I was hit on the forehead by a piece of shrapnel fired from the anti-aircraft gun on Penn Common.

I was a midwife from 1931 to 1965. I didn't want to retire, but people used to say, "It's about time you had a rest." In the end I took the hint. Even now, when it's quiet I think about some of the individual cases, the long or difficult labours. I'm not sentimental, but whenever I completed a satisfactory delivery, I used to say a little prayer under my breath, and of course, I would fret if something had not gone right. Looking back I am glad that I did something useful, and I'm glad that I enjoyed my work.

3

TRANSPORT

Wolverhampton's First and Last Woman Trolleybus Driver

Amy Davies

When I left school it was the time that Courtaulds and Goodyear were building new factories in Wolverhampton, but I went into domestic service as a maid. Years later, when I worked for the Corporation Transport, if someone passed some comment that implied they looked down on me, I was able to assure them that I had walked and talked with the highest in the land! The coming of the War put me out of my job. My boss, who had been in the Yeomanry, was called up. He no longer required a staff to look after his house, so we all lost our jobs.

Of course fellers were called up, but women were also directed to War Service. I was a little over the conscription age and was not sure what I should do when my sister sent me a paper stating that the Transport Department was recruiting women as conductresses. I was eventually called to an interview in Wolverhampton, and, although they were desperate for staff as so many men had joined the Forces, they started to query whether I could be relied on to turn up for work as I lived far away in the village of Little Saredon - way outside the Borough! Ironically, in all the years I worked for them I never let them down, or had much time off through sickness. They insisted that I obtain lodgings in the town. I did so - temporarily - but I hardly used them, as "home was best".

I travelled to work on my push bike, and later bought a motorbike, but I could not get enough petrol during the War to be able to use it every day. Late at night and early mornings I seldom saw anyone else on the road. It was cold on those early mornings when I had to start about half past five. It was very annoying to be stopped by a sentry as I passed over the Borough Boundary by The Peartree. At the point of his gun I would have to undo my mac, and remove my sheet of brown paper that I wore to protect myself from the wind, and find my ID card.

When I started as a conductress I worked on the Willenhall and Walsall route (5 and 5A). I got on well with the people on that route and enjoyed my work. At first the passengers occasionally had to help me with the fares and I dreaded having to cope with a full bus, but eventually I was able to take it all in my

Above: Amy Davies and trolleybus 437 at the Stone Street terminus, in Dudley, of Wolverhampton's 58 route, 5 March 1967. On that day the town's history of trolleybus operation came to an end. 437 was a Sunbeam vehicle built in Wolverhampton in the late 1940's, with Roe bodywork - similar to the vehicle preserved at the Black Country Museum.

stride. In the War years we never went out with an empty bus, it always seemed busy, a double decker bus carrying as many as we could get on.

If the bus seemed full but I stopped to squeeze one more person on I was the best friend he had ever had, but if my bus was so full one more person just could not be wedged in, I was that person's worst enemy! We were so busy that sometimes we had no time to eat our sandwiches, and meal breaks were unknown. Sometimes I had a cup of tea, sometimes not. But if a passenger saw me drinking tea he would be sure to say, "It's 'er - drinking tea again!"

About 1942 they called for women volunteers to take up trolleybus driving. They asked us to put in applications, but strangely enough, I never made an application, although an Inspector from Willenhall, on my route, was always nagging me to do so. I think they eventually gave up waiting for us to volunteer because a notice suddenly appeared containing a list of names of people directed to take up trolleybus driver training - and my name was on the list.

Inspector Tommy Lea began to instruct us, using single decker trolley buses driving round the Park Lane Depot. We learned about the wiring and electrics of a trolleybus and what to do in the event of a fire. We were soon plunged into putting our hands and feet onto the controls - and were expected to master the art of trolleybus driving within three days. We had to learn how to pull up alongside the curb, and how not to stray too far from the path of the overhead wires. Someone who had driven a petrol or diesel bus often found this quite hard to learn because they were used to being able to drive anywhere. If the trolley poles were pulled from the overhead wire it was called a "dewirement". Some of the smaller girls found that the tension in the poles was enough to lift them off the ground if they struggled to re-wire their trolleybus.

A blonde girl named Nancy Price and myself were the first to take our test. I passed out in the morning and she passed out in the afternoon, and by that fluke I had the distinction of being the first woman trolleybus driver in Wolverhampton. Nancy married one of the drivers from Bournemouth when some of their vehicles and drivers were sent to Wolverhampton to help us out. Eventually there were thirteen of us women drivers, but being on different routes and different shifts we could work for ages without seeing one another, but we had some happy times.

I drove my trolleybus on my Walsall route - perhaps making six or seven return trips in an eight hour shift, but, sadly that was one of the first routes on which trolleybuses were withdrawn. After the War it was touch and go if we could keep our jobs as the men started to come back. They had been promised their jobs, but, as it happened, they didn't want them, and we were left to trundle on. I was happy to continue because I like everything about driving, I was single, and I had to continue working for my living.

People used to say, "You want to get yourself a nice little cushy conducting job when they take the trolleys off." but I felt they could do what they liked with me - I wasn't going to apply for anything, I would just bide my time. When the last trolleys worked on the

Dudley route in 1967, I was working the mid-day shift on the last Sunday of operation. They didn't let me drive the last one in, or anything like that, but by working that day, I was Wolverhampton's last woman trolleybus driver, as well as its first.

I was pushed around anywhere and everywhere after the trolleys were taken off. I did some conducting, but it upset me to be working with a driver if his driving was bad - and some of them were awful. Even today I am considered very rude because I prefer to travel to town on the half-hourly Cannock bus rather than the West Midlands one - but on the Cannock bus the driver waits till I am sitting down before he drives off - which is the kind of thing that counts. What I really miss is a conductor to give me a shove up onto the bus!

I also worked in the Lost Property Department but I hated 9 till 5 work after working shifts. I found myself thinking that I only had four more years until my retirement, then, to my horror, I found that, as I had been doing a man's job, I would have to work until I was 65. Fortunately that changed and I was able to retire in 1973, after thirty three years service. I had never expected to stay for so long.

When I first started driving trolleybuses I was interviewed by the BBC Radio for the "Home News" - presumably to encourage other girls to take up such jobs. I still have the "script", passed by the censor, and dated 22 June 1942. When I drove my last trolley bus in 1967 it was fiercely being debated whether women should be allowed to drive diesel buses. I would have loved to have had a go, and with a pre-selector gearbox and power-assisted steering, I am sure I could have taken it in my stride.?

Wolverhampton Corporation Transport Department's lady trolleybus drivers, 1943. Left to right: (standing) Cissie Hallam, Betty Hill, Lily Hyde, L.J.Davies, Mary Sweetman, Lily Brookes and Ann Pringle. (Seated) Doris Cooper, Betty Wood, Amy Davies, Nancy Price, *and Winnie Perry. During the War, Wolverhampton's fleet was supplemented by some vehicles from Bournemouth. Nancy Price, who had become a driver on the same day as Amy, married one of the Bournemouth drivers. (Amy Davies' collection)*

Working with Jack

Phyllis Rudd

Before the War I was working at Heath's fruit shop in Stafford Street, Willenhall. In those days oranges arrived in barrels, and potatoes were in hundredweight sacks - not half a hundredweight like they are today. Working in a fruit shop was heavier than you might think, but it was all good training for my future work. I remember bananas arriving in big wooden crates, and they were packed in straw. We opened these crates very gingerly because we never knew what might jump out of the straw!

I worked with a girl from Wolverhampton and she told me that there were vacancies for guards on the passenger trains. We liked the idea of that kind of job and she went off to make enquiries, but they were all taken. I ended up working for the railway, not as a guard, but as a worker in the goods yard - working alternate weeks at Bilston Street and Stafford Street yards in Willenhall, on the LMS.

I bought myself bib and braces to go to work, but the railway eventually issued us with denim jackets and trousers, and a cap that we never wore. I wished I had kept my denims - they issued us with several sets - they would have been worth a lot today! I was nineteen years old when I started, and I found myself working with twenty other women, of all ages, recruited for work in the yards. Men and women worked together well, and the older men usually had to teach us the jobs. The men had serge uniforms that must have been very hot to wear in the summer.

I began by unloading the railway trucks, and filling the drays for the drivers. Much of it was heavy work unloading steel and pig iron, but my experience in the fruit shop had prepared me well. It took three of us to lift a bar of steel and throw it on the dray, and it had to be handled carefully or you could easily smash a finger. On two occasions I smashed my wedding ring on my finger - these things happened, but we soon got over them. We used to load wagons with ammunition boxes and I used to clamber up great piles of them, but I couldn't do it now! And there was always fun to be had in loading American jeeps, because you never knew what you might find in them!

Eventually the Station Agent, Mr.A.Homer, asked me if I would consider driving a horse and dray. The strange thing was that I was terrified of horses. I think I had learned this fear when I was a child. I had memories of the big black horses with plumes that were used at funerals. Those horses used to pound their feet on the road in a manner that was frightening. A year after I started working for the railway I had married, and my husband had joined a cavalry regiment, so I suppose it was appropriate for me to learn to work with horses.

The first day out with a horse and dray I was accompanied by an older regular driver, who was to provide me with some training, and to show me what to do. Mr.Pinson was a good trainer, and he showed me how to put the horse into the shafts of the dray, and how to fasten him up. Then I was shown the rounds; where to pick up, and where to deliver, the goods. Horses are intelligent animals and usually know where they are going and where to stop.

The railway employed an ostler at the station to look after the horses, and he had the horse ready for me when I arrived each morning, and all I had to do at the end of the day was return the horse to the stable. I soon became used to handling the horse during the day, and overcame my fear of them, and loved the job. My horse was called Jack, and I think I worked with him for all but a couple of days of my service with the railway. A driver could develop a relationship with the horse. I remember a little lady called May Dunkley who took over a huge black horse from Mr.Lewis. That horse was called Ben - and he pulled his heart out for her.

Jack was usually very amenable and good-natured. However, on one occasion he suddenly kicked up his feet and away he went. I was perched on a little flat box on the floor of the dray, but I managed to haul him back - so much that he almost sat on his backside. He tried it again one other time, and ran from the clock, down the hump-backed bridge, round the corner and straight down the yard to the stables. I was terrified stiff. Mr.Pinson drove into the yard behind me, saying, "Are yo' all right, my wench?" I felt that I could have been killed. The men must have known that Jack could occasionally behave like that, but no-

body had warned me. Jack never behaved that way again, for which I was very grateful.

We used to deliver to local factories from the Stafford Street station, and to local shop goods and around the town from Bilston Street. The steel and pig iron, which was heavy, used to go to John Harper, and to another little factory that used to be at the end of New Road: Horton & Smith. The driver who made the last delivery of pig iron of the day was always given sixpence, so everybody in the yard used to be shouting, "I want that load, I want that load!" Mind you, after working in the shop where I had earned 12/6 a week, I couldn't believe my first week's wages when I joined the railway.

I enjoyed the work because I felt I was a "free agent" when out on my round, and I liked meeting people. I met nice people and funny old folks. The first summer I was out with Jack the weather was beautiful, and even if I had to work in the yard, I was still out in the fresh air, which was what I liked. On one occasion when I was not working with Jack, I was given a horse that looked more like a race horse than a cart horse. He wouldn't stop when we came to the end of one street, and one of the few cars that were about came right across our path. The driver shouted, "Don't you know your Highway Code?"
"Yes I do," I replied, "but I'm sorry that the horse doesn't!"

As well as driving the horse and dray, I trained in a variety of other jobs. For example, I did number-

Below: Three forms of propulsion can be found in this mid 1920's picture of the LMS railway goods yard at Ettingshall (Ketchem's Corner). On the left is a 1924 AEC 2 ton flatbed petrol lorry with solid tyres. On the right are horse drawn drays, and in the distance a steam traction engine appears to have brought a Thompson boiler into the yard. The drivers are wearing aprons, the lorry driver sports a jacket, collar and tie, and the figure in the distance, in a double-breasted serge coat, may be the goods agent.

checking. This entailed a very pleasant walk down to the trucks each morning, and before they were shunted into the yard I had to check details of where they had come from, what they were carrying, and to whom the goods was consigned - after first taking the number of the truck. I had a good memory for recalling trucks, and their position, which was useful if there was a query.

I also dealt with special loads that had to put into wagons on their own. Sometimes such loads needed "scotching" - packing with blocks to prevent movement, and sometimes a load had to be sheeted over, and then a ticket had to be made out recording details of the consignment. Sometimes we were so busy in the yard that part-time folk had to come in and help during their time-off, as part of their contribution to the War Effort. Occasionally there were arguments, but I always acted on my orders from the Yard Foreman.

On Saturdays we finished work at lunchtime, and we used to go to the pub on the bridge - The Dog & Partridge. One of the women could play the piano, so we had a couple of drinks and a sing-song for an hour. And that was that for another week, until starting work on Monday morning again. I don't remember any other social life, but we enjoyed each others' company, and worked well together. Many of my colleagues were older than me, but I still see them about now and again when shopping, or on the bus. When we meet we like to talk about the old days.

I was asked if I would like to train for lorry-driving work, and after I was twentyone I was taught to drive a two ton Dennis flat-back lorry. My instructor was always worried about something - "Watch your tyres, watch this, watch that.." But I passed my test first time. Then I learned to drive a Scammell three-wheel

tug, and passed my test first time again. Having passed my tests, I was never asked to take a lorry out, although I used to drive them within the yard. I also trained in fog signalling. An old man who lived in one of the cottages by the hump-back bridge showed me how to place detonators on the track - but, again, I was never called out to do it.

The railway gave us one free ticket a year, and four quarter fares, and I found that very useful after the War when my husband was in hospital in Liverpool, after returning from North Africa. I left the railway to have my children but went back after the birth of the first and second, but not the third. Times were changing, and I could see new bigger lorries replacing the older ones, and the horses and their drays began to fade away. I was never able to take my children down to the yard to see the horses that I had worked with. Since that time I have worked in shops, markets and factories - I like being with people and being out and about - so sometimes I wish those days were back again.

The vehicles pictured on the opposite page were engaged in short haul traffic, but the period between the Wars also saw the development of the motor lorry for long distance work. Below: A pre-War view of Wright Brothers' vehicles and drivers at their Crown Street, Wolverhampton, garage. The building itself survives, and Claude Wright, on the extreme right of the picture, is still alive today. John Spittle, who describes his driving career overleaf, gained experience driving Wrights' trucks. On the left is an Atkinson, on the right a Foden of the early 30's, and in the centre, a Foden of the late 30's. (John Spittle Collection)

WE ARE AT YOUR SERVICE·   P.T.O.

Above: John Spittle now builds beautiful models of heavy commercial vehicles after years of drinving them! Using card and scrap materials, he has built accurate models of many vehicles used locally, including this West Bromwich built Jensen operated by R & L Horton of Lower Gornal.

Driving

John Spittle

In the late twenties, when I was about six years old, my father bought me my first pedal car, and from that time on I have always been interested in anything on wheels. We lived in a bungalow on the Stafford Road. At the time it was the only building between the ECC, at Dunstall, and the Vine, at Fordhouses, and my Father was running his own business in milk haulage - long before the famous firm of Myers was established in Wolverhampton.

My Father had seen some milk churns at a railway station, and decided that carrying milk in churns by rail was a slow and expensive way of doing the business. He bought himself a lorry on hire purchase and started carrying milk. He was joined by his brother, and they had a Chev and a Bean, which they worked for a number of years. This was during my early childhood, when there were still trams in Wolverhampton, and I can remember the Brooke Bond Trojan vans getting stuck in the tram tracks! A trolley bus route was opened to Greenwood Road where they turned round by the Goodyear on the Stafford Road.

My great Grandmother's second husband was Godfrey Frederick Bauer, a German, who had started a business in Crown Street manufacturing sausage cas-

ings. I started working for Bauer Casings when I was about thirteen, and later my family became more involved in the business. Mr. Bauer was interned during the Second World War, so we had to help out. Later, when he died, my great Grandmother persuaded my Father to sell his milk wagons and go into the business. My Father was great friends with Claud Wright of the Wright Brothers who ran a haulage business in Crown Street. The two men were never too busy to help each other, and my first lorry driving experience was probably on their yard. During the War, if one of Claud Wright's men failed to report for work, we could usually help out.

I was certainly ready to apply for my driving licence as soon as I was seventeen in 1939, while working at Bauer Casings. The strange thing is that just as I fixed my L plates to the truck, wartime regulations came into effect and I never used my L plates, or took a test! I simply went to the Tax Office next to the Civic Hall, handed over my five shillings and was issued with a licence in the interests of "The Defence of the Realm".

My pride and joy when driving for Bauer Casings was the American Ford, but I also drove the Wright Brothers' trucks - taking the self-sealing tanks for the Lancaster Bombers up to Metro Vickers, or going to the Spitfire works at Squires Gate. I was in my late teens, and we certainly had some fun on the road. And I was never short of company, as I never refused anyone a lift. There were hard times, like sitting outside Liverpool docks all night frozen to your seat, but scared to move in case someone pinched your place, but the job also gave me a chance to see inside naval yards, submarine yards and power stations that the normal citizen never had the chance to see.

My great Grandmother died a few years after the War, and we did not inherit the business. In fact by 1951 I found myself put out of work, so I went to the newly formed British Road Services in Jenner Street. They gave me a job straight away, and I was put in an old Bedford and sent off to London. As a result of Nationalisation, BRS found themselves with all the old rubbish from all over the place, and the Bedford was terrible.

After unloading in London, I had to collect a load of tyres in Kent, and bring them back to Shrewsbury. The truck had broken down about fourteen times by the time I came to a halt near the Ford factory at Dagenham: the axle shaft had broken. I had had enough. I went to the phone box and rang the nearest BRS depot and told them, "Your vehicle is outside Ford's at Dagenham, but I ain't." Then I hitch-hiked back to Wolverhampton, and a Star Aluminium lorry from Graisley got me home by midnight.

I drove for Contactor Switchgear for a few years, and then took a fortnight's work at Goodyear's as a Relief Driver during the holiday period. I did well, and I was the steady kind of bloke they wanted - not the sort of bloke to give them a lot of mouthy back-chat - so I stayed for ten years with never a complaint!

Goodyear's was a smashing firm to work for, and I only left because a new test truck arrived and I was determined to drive it! The work on this truck turned out to be shift work and that didn't suit me. Even so, I drove the test truck for twelve months. It was in use twenty four hours a day, and its brakes never had the chance to cool. One night they asked me to

Above: John Spittle and the American Ford owned by Bauer Casings Company of Wolverhampton, in the 1940's. In the background are the houses of the Fallings Park Garden Suburb on the Cannock Road. (John Spittle Collection)

take it out, having arranged for the brakes to be looked at by the Leyland place on the Birmimgham New Road. I wasn't too happy about it, but I had never refused to do a job, so off I went.

On the Shrewsbury Bypass I was forced off the road to avoid a car, and as we sank onto the soft verge, the truck almost turned over. Somehow we came out of it all right but I knew then that I had had enough of the shifts and this particular truck, so I left Goodyear's. As I walked out past the Gatehouse, I said to the lads, "When I come back in here, I'll buy you all them wagons and trailers, and find jobs for the best of you." Years later I bought ten vehicles off them. I didn't entice their drivers away, but my old mates used to drive for me in their holidays - so I was true to my word.

I started up on my own with one Bedford, and gradually built up my own fleet buying one or two more at a time. For ten years I drove them night and day all over the country - and eventually sold them for more than I had paid for them in the first place! My life was made easier when the Labour government abolished the old system of A,B and C licences. The new law took effect from midnight, and I was ready loaded up in my Bedford - ready to depart for Norwich at 1.a.m.: my first trip in my own wagon: 150. My wagon was only an old "rubber", but I had painted it beautifully and it looked nice, it went well, and I did what I'd got to do, so plenty of work came my way.

Building up the business wasn't easy. Sometimes I would go to my lorry in the morning and find my tyres let down. One morning I found a spike driven through the fuel tank. And I didn't find that all transport managers were honest men. Trying to set up your own haulage business could mean paying a backhander to such folk just to get the work, but even then they would

give the work to someone else who could come along with a bigger bribe. In my first Bedford I can remember completing a round trip to London with only three gears, two forward gears and reverse, because I feared losing the work if the trip was not undertaken.

I thought nothing of driving to Glasgow and back without stopping. The wipers could be going back and forth all the way, leaving me with a headache that lasted a fortnight, but it was a life of adventure, usually enjoyable and interesting. My vehicles were my pride and joy. I had no children so I devoted my life to them - I was never out of my overalls. I loved driving them, maintaining them, painting them in my own orange and blue livery, even doing the loading and unloading. I never employed strangers, I only took on men that I knew, and I was happy working with them. I traded for about sixteen or seventeen years, and eventually had a fleet of about twelve vehicles.

I taught myself painting and signwriting and prided myself on having spotless vehicles. Whenever I see a Jensen lorry I am reminded of what became of one of my spotless lorries. One night I was coming up the M1 when I was overtaken by a Jensen carrying barrells of paint. I said to a young lad in the cab with me, a chap called Derek, "We'll still be home before he is." And sure enough about seven miles futher on we found he had become involved in an accident, and the paint was forming a great lake across the motorway. We drove past without stopping, but when I saw the motor in the light of the next day it looked like ten zebras! My tyres were psychedelic and paint covered every part of the chassis and the underside of the wings. It was a high price to pay for getting home first.

Over the years my lorry driving life caught up with me. I had been driving since I was seventeen, through the years of the Wartime "Black-out", years of being in draughty cabs with horrible seats, often wet through and cold. I began to suffer from "lorry-drivers' disease" - lumbago. For twenty five years it had gradually got worse, but I couldn't give up driving.

Then an attack of shingles put me on the settee for seven and a half months. I couldn't move, and could do nothing but lay on my back and watch vapour trails in the sky. Arthritis of the spine set in and I was sent to see various specialists. One specialist - a real refined gent in a white gown - saw me at the hospital in Bath Avenue. He said,
"Well Mr. Spittle, I understand that you drive lorries?"
"Yes."
"They're your own aren't they?"
"They're nobody else's - there's only my name on the licence."
"Well, I'm afraid your days of driving trucks are finished. If you carry on you will end up in a wheel chair for the rest of your life."
I thought to myself, I've got an HGV Class 1 licence, but I don't know what sort of licence I'd need for a motorized wheel chair - but I certainly don't want one!

So thats how I finished. Of course,I had a team of drivers, but how can you ask people to do what you can't do yourself. When I sold the trucks, I kept one of the tractor units and I would rather drive that than drive a car, but really I would rather walk to town today than drive at all.

Trucks are still my life, and I spend my time building models of them. There is great satisfaction to be had from working in plastic sheet with just a craft knife, and making accurate models of these vehicles. I can't be persuaded to part with any of them, and there are always people begging me to make a model of their particular truck. I'm sixty eight now and if I build models for another ten years I won't satisfy everybody.

Waiting on the Rank

Steral Williams

Driving a cab is a funny business. I sit around for half an hour or more waiting for a fare, and after all that waiting maybe someone climbs into my cab who only pays a pound or one pound fifty for their journey, but you never know what might happen next, you never know when you might be lucky. When I think about my life it seems strange that I have changed my job almost by accident at times when I didn't know what was coming next. I've been a cautious sort of chap, almost a "stick-in-the-mud", and now I'm doing a job where I never know where my next passenger might want to go!

I worked on the railway for thirteen years. It was work on the track and it was very poorly paid, but I worked hard and never missed a day if I could help it because I believed that my kids should never go hungry, that they should be well clothed, and have the chance to take advantage of education. I worked six days a week, often twelve hours a day, and somehow I was stuck in that job and did not look for anything else.

For the last four months I was on the railway, I was a wagon and carriage examiner at Bescot. The journey from my home in Wolverhampton to Bescot was so awkward that I had to have a car for the journey. One Saturday morning I was taking the Missis shopping in Wednesfield when the back spring broke as we were driving along. Suddenly there was no way that I could report to Bescot at 6.00.am on Sunday morning, but it was one of those accidents that changed my life.

Having failed to report for work on the Sunday, I set out on Monday morning to see if I could find a job nearer home. I ran into my friend Phillip and said, "How about a job at the place where you are working?" and to my surprise he told me to go along with him the next day. And that's how I came to work at Bean's.

Left: John Spittle, in his BRS cap, alongside a Bedford articulated lorry in Goodyear's fleet. (John Spittle's Collection)

I told the boss that I had never worked in a foundry but he still took me on - and I stayed there for six years. When I received my first wages I discovered I was earning twice what I had earned on the railway. After thirteen years of hardly being able to buy myself a pint, I found, within three years, that I was able to start buying a house!

In 1979 I was made redundant from the Bean, in Tipton, but this time I couldn't find myself another job anywhere. I was out of work for four and a half years and was desperate for another break. Eventually one came. My daughter used to live in Showell Road next door to an Indian chap with a black cab. His name was Mack, and he worked in a factory by day and drove the cab at night. My daughter said to him, "How come your cab is parked all day doing nothing?" and he explained that he had no-one to drive it. "Well my Dad is a good driver - he's been driving for years and he's never had an accident," said my daughter. Mack simply said, "Well, tell him to come down and see me."

Mack explained everything to me, and told me how to go about getting a taxi-driver's badge, and how to go for the test, so I went to the Council to apply for the licence. Really I was fortunate once again, because I didn't realise that I was supposed to know every street in Wolverhampton. I was not properly prepared for the test, but the chap from the Council asked me to take him to Merryhill and to various streets in that area. Somehow I found them, so I was given the badge. I gather the test is more difficult now!

I'm sure I would have gone crazy if I had remained unemployed, so I was pleased that Mack had given me the chance to drive his cab during the day. Yet the funny thing was that I didn't like the job at first. I hated the waiting for passengers, and the uncertainty of not knowing whether you might earn £1.50 or £15 on your next trip. But the Missis and the kids used to say to me, "Dad, you've been without a job for such a long time - you'd better try and get used to it!"

After eighteen months I had adjusted to it, and discovered that I greatly preferred driving a cab to working in a factory. Now I wish that I had always done it, ever since coming to this country. What I like is the feeling that I am my own boss. In the factory I felt I had to watch every move I made - one wrong move and I could be sacked.

Once I started to like the job, I decided that I would like to buy my own cab. Of course all my savings had dwindled away while I had been out of work, so I decided to go to Jamaica to try and raise some money. I went to see my seven brothers and they helped me, so that when I returned to Wolverhampton I was able to set out on my own. As well as people running their own cabs, there are two companies in Wolverhampton that run black cabs: Associated and Arrow, and by having a radio they will direct you to your next fare, in return for a weekly fee, but I decided not to bother with a radio, so I just wait at the ranks.

One disadvantage of having the radio is that you can be sent on "dead jobs". This occurs when someone maliciously phones the company who then radio the driver. When the driver goes to the caller's address he finds that nobody lives there, or no-one has called a taxi. By working from a rank regularly, I have gradually got to know most of the people who use cabs, and they know me. And I am lucky - because I meet more nice people than nasty people.

When the drivers get together they swop stories. We like to tell other drivers if things have gone well. For example, we may have picked up a Japanese industrialist from Wolverhampton Station, and run him out to Telford and been given a good tip. It's always nice when you get a tip - it makes your day. We don't like to dwell on the less pleasant things that can happen, and the chance we are taking every time we pick up someone.

Once I was thumped without even leaving the rank. Six blokes climbed into my cab just before Christmas. I told them I was only licenced to carry five but they

Right: Steral Williams and his Austin taxi at the rank, Market Street, Wolverhampton, in the summer of 1990.

swore at me and called me names. I left my steering wheel and went round and opened the door and told them that one guy would have to get out and board the next taxi in the rank. As I walked away I felt someone thump me three times. Eventually the Police arrested him and he was charged with assault, but that demonstrates the kind of thing that can happen.

We very rarely refuse to give people a ride, but just occasionally a passenger is so drunk we don't want to help - but that's basically because they are so drunk that they don't really know where they want to go! Often a person climbs into the cab without us looking at them. Once I looked round as we stopped at the first set of lights and found that my passenger was covered in blood pouring from wounds. He wouldn't let me take him to the hospital - and I was worried about bloodstains on my cab!

About four o'clock one afternoon, two Christmases ago, I was coming back from Tettenhall. I was coming up the Newhampton Road through Whitmore Reans and was flagged down by a young chap. I thought he was taking advantage of our "Flag a Cab" Rule, and that I was about to earn 50p for taking back to the nearest rank, but as he climbed in he said, "Can you take me to Scunthorpe?"

I said, "Come on, guy, you must be joking. Do you know where it is?" (I didn't know where it was myself.) He said, "Head for Nottingham, then Doncaster, and we'll get there." I found a driver with a radio and he asked Associated what would be the fare to Scunthorpe? They told us it would £85. When I heard that, I suggested that he went by train, but he insisted that he just wanted to get home for Christmas.

I told him that he would have to pay part of the fare before we set out. He gave me £20, which was all he had, and we set out. It was a chance that I wouldn't take again, but when we reached his home his parents were so glad to see him that they paid the fare, and I set off again for Wolverhampton. It was half past one when I arrived home - eight hours extra driving after I had almost finished my day's work - it knocked me up for the rest of Christmas.

Times are hard now, and its a struggle to make a living. I have to pay my own insurance, pay garage repairs on the taxi and keep it going. I am fifty now, and my kids have grown up. When I was younger I thought nothing of working fourteen or sixteen hours a day, but now ten or twelve hours a day is enough. Once there was great competition in the taxi business, but now I think we realise we are all in the same struggle to earn some bread. We always give each other a wave, and I think we work well together - I don't even feel any great animosity for our rivals, the "private hire" drivers.

I'm having strong feelings about going home. This country doesn't need us any more, unless we have special skills. Of course, there is hardship and unemployment in Jamaica, and therefore it can be very difficult to know what to do in the future. Life is a big gamble anyway, and I have learnt to live with not knowing what is going to happen next.

Welcome to Stafford Road

Ken Southern

My experience of joining the Great Western Railway during the last War illustrates the way in which the railway recruited labour from the rural parts of England and Wales and brought such labour to work in areas like the industrial Midlands where young people were earning twice as much in the factories, or had joined the Forces. Our work was hard and dirty and there was one time when it seemed so bad that Jack Morris and I decided to join the Army. They wouldn't take us on - because of the Essential Works Order. We were trapped - we could neither seek better paid work, nor volunteer to fight for our country. We had to be railwaymen whether we liked it or not.

I was born and bred in Oswestry and, apart from agriculture, the town's only industry was the railway. That suited me because my goal was to become a railwayman. In 1942 I was given a job in the Road Motor Engineer's Department, concerned with the maintainance of railway vehicles. However, I was only there a few months when a railway employee who was invalided out of the Army took his job back, and made me redundant in that department.

They transferred me to the old Cambrian Railway Works as a "stick lad", and my job there was to make four hundred and forty firelighters per day. These box-shaped firelighters were made out of wood from chopped up railway sleepers and scrap wood from old wagon planks. Reclaimed dirty cotton waste was put inside them, and they were used for lighting the fires of steam locomotives at all the depots in the area, from Chester to Aberystwyth, and from Oswestry to Wolverhampton. My wage was 19/- a week, but the important thing was that the position represented one small step towards working on the footplate.

Eventually I left Oswestry to become an engine-cleaner at Shrewsbury, but within three months I was transferred back to Oswestry. Because of the Wartime Blackout regulations we cleaned engines in perpetual darkness. Fires had to be covered, and all light had to be concealed - the windows were blacked out and the vents were blocked. The air was full of dust and smoke. It was a drab and dreary environment, and we cleaned the engines with the oily cotton waste that later found its way into those firelighters. One thing to look forward to was the chance to do a few firing turns on the local shunting engines.

In peacetime progress to the footplate was slow, but a War was on, and at the age of seventeen I could apply to become a fireman. I was called to Swindon, and went through tests that lasted two days. The first day was basically a medical examination, and the second day was spent doing a practical test and an intelligence test. As far as the GWR was concerned, a test of whether you were intelligent enough to be a fireman or not was to find out if you were able to spell "vacuum". Every lad was despatched to Swindon with the advice, "Remember there are two 'U's in vacuum!"

Before I left Swindon I had to register, and be given my number. I had to pay 2/10d, in cash, at the desk, and this was my entrance fee to the Mutual Assurance Society, which was the GWR enginemen's pension fund. The number given to you on receipt of the fee, was a number that you had to carry with you all your

Right: Ken Southern on the footplate of ex GWR "King" class 4-6-0, 6005, "King George II". The "Kings" worked the Wolverhampton Low Level - Paddington expresses until 1962.

life - you would never forget it. My number is 31301. The number guaranteed that promotion strictly followed seniority - you could not be by-passed by someone with a higher number.

Your number was also used to allocate you to a shed, so I could have ended up anywhere on the GWR system. After returning to Oswestry, I was called to the office on Thursday afternoon and told that I had to report to Wolverhampton on Monday as a fireman. I felt very proud, and pleased that I was fulfilling my ambition.

Wolverhampton seemed a very big place to me and I knew that the shed was some way from the town centre. However, I had been advised that the locomotive uncoupled from the train at Wolverhampton Low Level station, and that it would then run back to the shed. I was told to tell the driver that I was a new fireman, and that he would give me a ride on the footplate to the shed. All this came true, and I was thrilled to ride on the footplate as we drove, tender first, back to the shed.

We stopped the engine on the turntable, as the fireman was washing himself down in a bucket of water. We walked from there to the shed itself, across a footbridge over the canal, and, as we did so, the fireman turned to me and said, "Well son, I don't know what you think you are doing coming here, but you'll be better off throwing yourself into that water!" That was my introduction to Stafford Road.

When I arrived in the office I found that I was one of eighteen lads starting that day. The clerk and the shed messenger were bustling around trying to give everybody directions to different parts of Wolverhampton to enable us to go and search for our own lodgings. I was sent to Low Hill, and went from door to door trying to find somewhere to live in this strange and busy town that already seemed full of people who had come from all over the place to work here. Many

lads were not successful and were given temporary accommodation by sympathetic footplatemen.

I found a place where I was offered a room for £2.50 a week - equal to half the sum of money I earned for six days work. I was shown to the small box room of a three-bedroom council house, and in there I was given a mattress, one sheet, and three overcoats! There were no canteens on the railway and the landlady was expected to provide me with sandwiches. This lady gave me four slices of bread and butter and a Midland Counties milk bottle full of cold tea each day.

One day, about four months later, I found that my money and my watch had gone missing. I mentioned this to a senior colleague who said, "Son, you haven't lost it - you've been robbed." He urged me to go to the police, but I was reluctant to do so. The following night the Foreman told me to go down beneath the arches of Oxley Viaduct - "You'll find two gentlemen in a car - they want to see you." It seemed strange but I followed the instructions, and the two men introduced themselves as detectives from Red Lion Street police station. They took down the details of what I had lost.

I was working on the night shunting locomotive at Herbert Street Goods Yard at the time, and generally finished about 4.00.am. I went home and went to bed. When I woke up my landlady was moaning that her husband hadn't come home from his nightshift, but I thought no more about it. I had to report back to work at 8.00.pm., only to find the two detectives waiting for me in Jones Road. To my amazement they showed me my watch, but they would not let me have it back, saying that I would have to come and identify it in court the next morning. So, I worked all night, and then went to court.

The magistrate was very shocked to hear how the railway had left us to fend for ourselves in finding somewhere to live. He wanted a full report from the

Above: Ken Southern (left) and Frank Wenman pose in front of the "Midland Pullman" at Cannock Road Carriage Sidings, Wolverhampton. The diesel "all Pullman" train service was introduced in 1960, by which time Ken was a diesel driver training instructor.

railway on the situation! Then the real shock came: when the thief was brought into the dock, he was my landlady's husband. I thought to myself, "Oh my God, it took me all day to find those lodgings - now I've lost them!" I went back to work that night feeling quite depressed that I would be homeless and would probably be in trouble with the railway for having brought their policies to the attention of the magistrate.

When I returned to the house the next morning, sure enough, there were two suitcases waiting on the doorstep - but they turned out not to be mine - they

One of the Wolverhampton based "Kings", 6011, "King James I", receives attention in the straight road shed at Stafford Road thirty years ago. (Simon Dewey)

were her husband's. She had thrown him out! Then the magistrate sent someone from the Council to find me some better digs. I moved to Kempthorne Avenue, and my whole life changed, because my new landlady, Mrs.Bristow, was very good to me. Everything was different. I had new clothes and a clean bed.

I have explained all this to show how a seventeen-year-old lad, recruited in the country, fared on the railway at the time. Later canteens and approved lodgings were introduced. What about life on the footplate? One of the features of starting work at Wolverhampton was that we were sent to Wednesbury for about eight weeks on the shunting engines. We even had to pay our own fare to and from Wednesbury: a privilege ticket cost us 18/- for three months. While we were there we were given a "mess room" that was an old horsebox with a gas lamp in it. It was just a rat-infested hovel, standing at the top of "the Farm", the exchange sidings between the GWR and the LMS, worked by three engines and their crews.

As a fireman I had visions of travelling from Lands End to John O'Groats on all kinds of trains, but after working at Wednesbury, I was sent to Oxley Shed and the reality was that we had to do some very hard and dirty work in the "Prep" and "Shunting" links. Due to the acute Wartime shortage of locomotives, trains were always waiting for one. As soon as a locomotive dropped onto the shed it had to be prepared immediately to go out on another job. We worked twelve hours on and twelves hours off, often seven days a week, for two years, preparing engines for their next duty.

Fires were cleaned and the engine was re-coaled, and the locomotive was handed to the men in the "Prep" link. The fireman's duty was to check the coal, and check that the fire had been re-lit in the correct manner. I had to check the sandboxes and top them up, examine the smokebox and tubeplates and tighten everything up. I had to assist the driver with the oiling and then sweep the cab out, trim the coal in the tender,

and crack the coal into lumps the correct size. Another job we did was called "cleaning the front". The regulator and steam pipes on the front of the footplate were always filthy and dusty, and we cleaned them off with thick black engine oil. The theory, handed down over the years, was that dust would stick to the oil, and that a cleaner environment would prevail on the footplate.

We worked on everything from tank engines to "Castles", and on a twelve hour shift we prepared eight locomotives. The strange thing was that no matter how dirty the job was, it was never grim, because we enjoyed the comradeship of the people with whom we were working. We went to work for the sheer pleasure of having the company of our own kind, and we would book-on early just to be there exchanging stories and laughter. As I said at the beginning, the one time that we did get fed up with it all, we discovered there was no escape. Most of the time we still felt we had a good job.

The one real escape from "Prep" work was the chance of a firing turn on one of the shunting engines. At Oxley Yard there were two engines at the north end - the Birkenhead engine and the Crewe engine, and two at the south end - the London engines, plus a utility engine to cope with anything that cropped up, and an engine that relieved the shunters. The yard was so busy that these engines never stopped work. Even the men, the shunters, came out and exchanged poles in the yard, as the engine paused to take water. There were no breaks. It was bang bang, shunt, shunt, all round the clock.

Eventually I progressed to the "Bank" link and worked the local freight trains from Oxley out to Buildwas in one direction, and to Handsworth & Smethwick in the other. I finished up firing for a driver who changed my life altogether. Up until that time my life had just been work and bare existence, with just enough money to keep my head above water. Through Walter "Titch" Aulton, I began to see life differently. During the four years that we worked together I learnt about the comradeship that can make a fireman and driver work as one. He was the "captain of the ship", but he taught me how to be a good fireman, and he befriended me at the same time. I was fulfilling my ambition and learning to take a pride in my craft. We had some wonderful experiences, and perhaps that is why the lad from Oswestry is still working on the railway in Wolverhampton today - nearly fifty years later.

Working in the Passimeter

Jack Winship

Like many of my generation, I was released from the Forces after the War without any marketable skills, but with a wife and family to support. I went to Cannon Industries as a millwright, and became Safety Officer, but then I went to Rubery Owen's Research and Development Department. I found myself helping to perfect a hop-picking machine. It was a wonderful machine and had to be modified left right and centre, but eventually we cracked it. After many

Above: Running a railway is a serious business! Even so, several parcels porters at Dudley Port seem to have found time to pose on the signal guarding the approach to the station from the Dudley line, in the early 1960's. Signals, gasworks, and houses have disappeared - but the tower of Tipton Library, just visible on the right skyline, has survived. (Cyril Hand)

hours out at Ledbury on various estates, we produced the machine that could pick hops. After that the work became rather boring, and I left to go to Henry Hope's where they were making metal windows. I didn't last long there either. About that time I saw an 'ad' in the paper saying they wanted booking clerks on the railway.

It didn't sound as if there would be much money in working for the railway but I thought I would give it a try. I was granted an interview at New Street, and saw the Staffing Officer, Charley Key, and he gave a quick mental arithmetic test, some columns of figures to add up, and asked me to write an essay. I had just read an article in the Daily Mail about pre-historic cave paintings and that provided the inspiration for my essay.

As a result I was offered a job, and was told there was a vacancy at Dudley Port, which I was very glad to have. I went along to Dudley Port and reported for duty. I was made very welcome, and everybody was very pleasant. I was put alongside an established clerk, Jack Evans, to learn the job. At the time there were three clerks: Jack Evans, George Coleman, and

Above: Parcels porters and Inspectors outside the Porters' Room on the up platform of Dudley Port Station in the early 1960's. Second from the left: Jack Salter, and the Inspector on the right is thought to be Bob Stanley. Unfortunately no photograph of the "passimeter" at Dudley Port has been found. (Cyril Hand)

George Cleaver. George Coleman, the Station Master's clerk was on the "Middle Turn" and dealt with all the parcels and wages and salaries. He worked gentlemanly nine-till-five hours. George Cleaver was the Head clerk, and was a little wisp of a man who looked like something out of Dickens. He wore the shabbiest suits I had ever seen, and carried a million pins in his lapel and six pens and pencils in his pocket. He had a shock of pan-scourer hair, and used to perch on his stool like a goblin, clutching his pipe with his two top teeth. He really went back to the old days - he was an ex LNWR man, and although formidible at first, he was really a very pleasant man. There was no Station Master because the post was vacant. We couldn't get one for ages as there wasn't a house available to go with the job. The only house on the station was down on the Low Level, and that was occupied by Ernie Moulton, who was the Station Master at Owen Street.

Dudley Port may be a lonely windswept platform crowned with a "bus shelter" today, but in the ten years I was there, from about 1950 to 1960, it was a busy place and it was a Class 1 station. This was helped by Palethorpe's - from whom we earned about £3000 per day for the carriage of sausages. The station was a hive of activity with four clerks, a Station Master, three Station Inspectors, three shunters, at least six parcels porters and various juniors, females and lampmen, three signalmen and the staff from Watery Lane and Albion. There was a staff of about sixty people. When I worked the middle turn and had to prepare the wages bill, I relied on working Sundays to get the job done for despatch at 4.00.pm Monday.

The Early turn was from 5.45.am to 1.45.pm and the Late Turn was from 3.05.pm to 12.45.am. after the Down Scot had gone through, which was always late. Charley had done me a good turn. There was so much overtime to work that I found I had a well paid job. Even in 1951 I was earning up to £36 per week - it was enormous dough! The Station Master didn't work overtime - so I was earning more than he did,

and I worked so many hours that I didn't have time to spend it. All along the line the richness of the blokes at Dudley Port was a legend. The money wasn't sent to the station to pay everybody. We received an authority which enabled us to withdraw the money from Barclays Bank in Great Bridge. We had to go and collect it "secretly" at the same time, and by the same route, each week.

At Dudley Port the station was up above your head as you approached it from Station Drive. There was a lift, an old foyer to the station, and beyond was the old parcels office which had burned down. In the booking office was a passimeter - a cell about ten foot by six foot in which we worked, and which could be passed on either side. The idea was that the booking clerk could collect tickets as well as sell them, from the same position, just as if you hadn't enough to do, with phone enquiries, covering for vacances, and doing the salary bills and traffic books all at the same time. In theory the clerk operated a treadle that opened a gate for passengers to pass through, but during my time a brick was placed on the treadle to keep the gates permanently open. You can imagine a football crowd coming back from the Wolves. There was no time to inspect each ticket as they came through. They simply poured past, throwing all sorts of things into the passimeter as they went by.

Saturday afternoons could be very lively if local football teams were playing at home. The Wolves supporters caught the 2.03. down Manchester train, while Villa supporters waited on the up platform for the 2.10. departure to Birmingham. From the Low Level a 1.55. "Special" would take the Albion supporters to the Hawthorns for 1/- return. I could take £70 in one shilling tickets in just a few minutes. You had to be pretty good at banging the tickets through the date press without catching your thumb in its jaws.

Nearly every train, except the down Holyhead express, stopped at Dudley Port, and one reason for this was that New Street was an "Open Station", without ticket collectors. Up expresses paused at Dudley Port so that tickets could be inspected. As the train arrived, the travelling ticket inspector would be leaning out of the train to signal to us how far down the train he had reached, and our staff would dive on and collect or punch the rest.

The variety of tickets we stocked was colossal. There were hundreds of catagories apart from destinations: singles, ordinary returns, monthly returns, bulk returns, issued on a warrant, workmans' returns, replaced by early morning returns, cheap day returns, special day returns, half-day excursions, forces' leave, theatricals and commercial travellers - all in first and third class. This is not to forget blind persons and their attendants, (Mr.Preedy, the local tobacconist, bought them) and tickets for dogs, cycles and prams (accompanied).

There were also "blanks" on which the clerk had to write out the destination. If a Tipton girl started courting some chap who lived on a remote part of the railway system we did not fancy having to write out her ticket every Friday night. We would ask her how soon she intended getting married, and if it was a long way off, we would order some printed tickets for that destination.

We still had a few LNWR tickets, much sought after by collectors. We had a ticket collecting buff come to buy one. He begged me to let him have one but, unfortunateley, the only one we had left was a first class blank privilege ticket, available only to company servants upon payment by voucher. I would have been stripped of my buttons and shot at dawn if I had sold one of those to a member of the public, but he was most insistent that he should have one so I sent him to the Station Master. He found Ted Ash in the Round Oak, and must have bought him a drink or two, as Ted appeared and said, "Let's give this gentleman a ticket. Let's make it first class to Tipton Owen Street." It cost threepence, and Ted paid with a voucher, so the enthusiast got his ticket.

There were always plans being made to rebuild Dudley Port, which was forever an excuse for not painting it, so it became more and more delapidated. George Wigg, Dudley's M.P., used the station frequently. George was a good friend and could get things done. Other local "big-wigs" used the station, like the Hillmans, the leather people, and the Marshes of Marsh & Baxter, so everybody added their influence and eventually our station was repainted. When they arrived the painters painted everything, and we couldn't open a door or window after they had gone, and from

then on the station was painted with monotonous regularity - but it was too late: the woodwork had already gone rotten.

The station was very exposed to the weather, elevated high above the Great Bridge road, and it shared this isolation with the canal that ran alongside the railway. There were two sidings between the main-lines and the canal, and, one night, Kenny Hartley, the shunter put six wagons in the canal. Ted Ash came back from the Round Oak shouting, "Where are the wagons, Ken?", but Ken said, "I'm damned if I know - they were there when I started."

So I was lucky. my job on the railway had turned out to be well paid and was never boring. And clerical staff didn't have to wear a uniform or a smart suit. We could go to work in what we liked. You could wear your pyjamas if you wanted to. From our passimeter we met the famous folks who came to appear at Dudley Hippodrome, and the locals who kept our station busy, until the electrification came along and the station was rebuilt in its present form. About 1960 I departed for New Street, when I joined the District Passenger Manager's staff, and I finished up on the Divisional Manager's staff.

Below: A large sector of the Black Country's manufacturing industry was devoted to the production of transport products. Local companies built cycles, motor bikes, cars, commercial vehicles, aircraft, military vehicles etc. (See Jim Boulton's "Powered Vehicles Made in the Black Country", published by the Black Country Society, 1990) Railway locomotives were built by the GWR at Wolverhampton's Stafford Road Works until early in this century. Rolling stock was built at Old-bury and Smethwick. Wheels, axles, tyres, engines, electric motors, accessories and components are, or have been, made locally. The Patent Shaft & Axletree Co. in Wednesbury produced iron and steel, and used the steel to build transport products from bogies to bridges. In this picture, taken about 1905, of Patent Shaft's Old Park Works, the gentlemen are surrounded by bogie frames built for the railways of India.

4

THE LAUNDRY BUSINESS

The Black Country's past is so firmly associated with sweat, dirt and grime, it seems worth trying to comple ment that image by invoking memories of the work involved in removing all that dirt. In both foundry and laundry, the work was once very labour intensive, and the conditions could be as hot and wet in one as the other could be hot, dry and dust-laden.
Top: Wet cleaning in the old wash house at the Wolverhampton Steam Laundry in 1929.
Bottom: The hand - ironing room, 1929. (Both pictures: WSL collection)

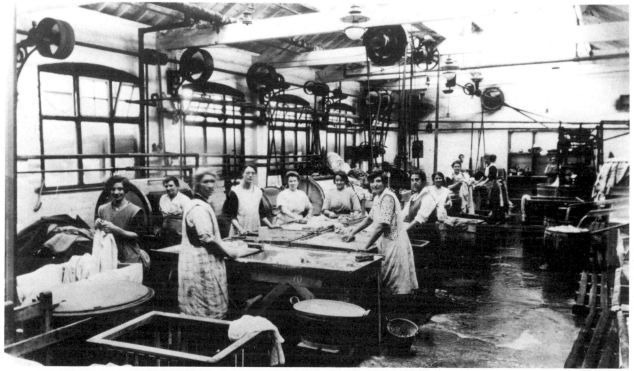

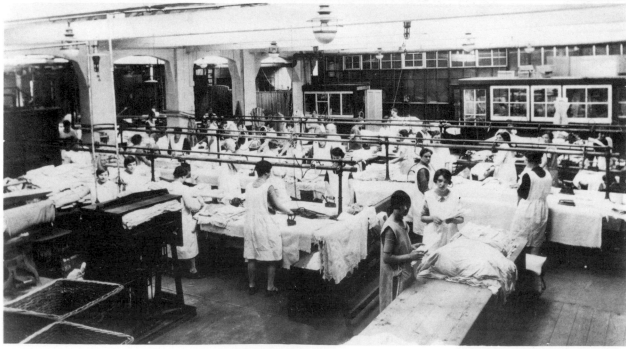

The Valeting Service

Clarry Siviter

My first job on leaving school was at T.W. Lench, Blackheath, for about six months. My father then found me a job at the Oldbury Carriage Works, but after a further six months the boss came round to where I was working:

"Clarence Siviter?"

"Yes"

"You're finished tonight."

My father had been stopped about one month before that, so we had no money coming into the house. It was imperative that I found another job.

I wandered around for a few weeks, and then I decided that I would go and try Cradley Heath Labour Exchange. Dad had to go to Oldbury exchange to sign on every week but I could go to any exchange in search of work as I was still under sixteen. At Cradley Heath they, in their wisdom, sent me to the Valeting Services, Newtown. I hadn't a clue where it was because outside Blackheath I was a lost soul, but I found it. I was told to report to a Mr. Hill, who, I later found out, owned the business jointly with his wife.

I walked up a drive to a little door. I opened it and poked my head in. the room was full of women ironing. A lady came over to me and asked me what I wanted, and then went away. Eventually Mr. Hill appeared. He was a small dapper immaculatley dressed man with a brisk manner, and he took me to a little office. I gave him the few details of my past history, and he decided to employ me - I don't know why - but he did. He wanted me to learn the whole concept of dyeing and dry-cleaning, and the pressing, and he wanted me to start on Monday morning. I walked home full of joy.

Monday morning arrived and I caught the bus from Blackheath down to Old Hill Cross. It was three pence - workman's return. Then I walked through the Sleepy Valley, through a disused farm yard, and over the pit banks into Newtown, for an eight o'clock start. As I turned into the road I could look down to the factory, and there I could see crowds of folks all standing around in groups. As I walked among them I could hear phrases like, "Ay, it was a blaze!" I thought to myself, "Blimey, there's bin a fire - this is where I don't start." I found Mr. Hill but he could only say, "Don't bother me now, come in tomorrow morning." I returned home not feeling very happy, nevertheless hoping that everything would be alright the next day.

The next day everything was fine. I learned that there had been a fire in the garage. It had burned the vans, and damaged the canteen above, but work could continue. Mr. Hill talked to me in the office and then took me into the Dry-Cleaning Department. It was not very big, and it was very clean, so it was unlike anywhere I had previously worked. I was introduced to Albert Hill, a young chap in his early twenties who turned out to be Mr. Hill's nephew.

Above: The "Hydro" - at Wolverhampton Steam Laundry, 1929: the equivalent of today's spin dryer. (WSL Collection)

Albert showed me the machines which I would have to load and unload, but the smell of the spirits used in dry-cleaning made me feel woozy, and then I felt ill. Albert told me to go outside in the fresh air to "clear my yed". I did so, and after a while the smell didn't matter, and really enjoyed working there. Albert also showed me an ingenious thing called the Clarifier - it was a French device through which the cleaning fluid passed to have the dirt removed from it. The fluid went through a tall cylinder which was spun round at a terrific speed, and all the dirt clung to a bowl inside it. Every so often we had to take the machine to pieces to extract the bowl to break the dirt off, using a leaded hammer and blunt chisel. The lumps of dirt were wrapped in newspaper and thrown in the boiler.

When the clothes had been cleaned in the machines, they were put into a trolley and taken to another machine which we called a "Hydro", but today we would call it a spin drier. We packed the clothes in, put a sheet over the top to stop them spinning out, and away she'd go. Then we took the clothes out and put them in a tumble drier for twenty minutes. None of the machines were self-driven, they were all belt-driven. The process was a little bit hit and miss, an "O.K. they're ready" kind of business. The clothes then had to be taken to the Sorting Department, where they removed any marks, or to the Press Shop.

The power to drive the machines came from a gas engine, and in the winter three of us had to start the engine. We had to pull a huge fly-wheel, about eight feet in diameter until it kicked off. Albert Evans, the Works Engineer, cum Electrician, cum Plumber, used to fiddle about with it, applying hot rags here and there, and we grunted and pulled until, all of a sudden, it clicked, shuddered, and away she'd go.

Our hours were fixed on paper, but not fixed in practice. You knew when to go to work, but what time you could go home was anybody's guess, and as the summer passed more and more work came into the factory. In the early thirties people would have their clothes cleaned rather than replace them, and the busiest time of year for doing this was certainly the summer. Once or twice I would go to work on a Monday, and not see my home again until Thursday night. Sometimes Mum had to bring me some food the next day - and meet me at the works gate. The men worked right through till late at night, then we would go up to the canteen and doss down in the lounger chairs - ready to dust our feathers at six the next morning, throw a bit of water in our faces, and return to work - we were that busy.

I remained in the Dry-Cleaning Department, and was joined by another young lad, Lionel White, which I felt entitled me to a move, but I stayed where I was. One day Miss Dovey, the company secretary, came in and said:
"Siviter? - Mrs. Hill wants to see you."
Albert looked at me, "What 'ave yo bin doin?"
"Nothing!"
He says, "Yo've got the sack."
I went off and waited in Mrs. Hill's office.
Mrs. Hill simply said, "You know where my car is?"
"Yes."
"Go and stand by it." And that was that.

When I reached the car I saw Lionel White walking up the yard as well, which made me think that perhaps things were not quite as bad as I first thought. When Mrs. Hill joined us we got into the car, without speaking, and drove away. We drove for about half an hour, into a world that I did not know existed - a world of country fields. I found out later that it was Hagley, and that was where the Hills lived.

We drove into their yard, got out, and walked into a marvellous orchard, full of apple trees. Mrs. Hill said, "Right, this is your job for two days. I want you to pick all the apples. don't bloody eat them and make yourselves ill." She seemed a very down-to-earth lady! Then she took us to the cook who was instructed to supply us with dinner. Then she said, "Right, you don't know how you're going to get back do you? Right - here's some money." She turned to me, "That's your bus fare to Stourbridge, and your train fare to Blackheath." Then she turned to Lionel, "That's your bus fare to Stourbridge and your train fare to Cradley Heath, and if you don't know your way - ask!"

The next day was the same. We had two marvellous days, and she allowed us to take quite a lot of apples home, which was a bonus. At other times, on Saturday mornings, I had to clean Mr. Hill's cream-coloured sports car. When I had finished he would come and inspect it, and if I had missed anything he would blow his top.

Eventually I moved to the Wet Cleaning Department, and there I met Joe Elwell, a Dudley man, uglier than Punch Joe, but with a heart of gold and a voice like a boy soprano. He had a beautiful voice, but he was as rough as a bear's bum. The third member of our team was Bernard, and we all wore clogs and aprons. Below our knees our trousers were saturated with water, and our clogs were full of water. Joe re-proofed the raincoats (it was the days of Swallow raincoats), and this was done in a huge tub of water, to which Joe added a solution of alum.

One day Joe appeared in a pair of Wellington boots - he had bought them himself. I looked at them with envy. Then Bernard bought some, but I could not afford them. One day, Mrs. Evans, the wife of of Albert the engineer, who was the lady in charge of the Press Shop, offered to loan me the money to buy some Wellingtons, paying her back a few pence a week. I thanked her but I was a rather silly proud lad and I refused the offer. I carried on, changing into old trousers when I came to work, taking my socks off, and wrapping old rags round my feet. My old trousers came from the "Unclaimed Goods" - which were normally sold to the employees.

I graduated from Wet Cleaning to the Dye House. There I worked with Bert Hardy, who reminded me of Oliver Hardy, and a bow-legged tough young Tarzan-like lad named Charly Harris. Soon after I started, Bert disappeared and was replaced with a vivacious curly-haired lad of about sixteen - the same age as myself. He was Bert Taylor, and the three of us got on like a house on fire. "The Desert Song" was popular at the time, and the three of us could sing well. In fact, Bert was in the Colley Gate Methodist Choir. We had huge boxes full of boiling dye, and an old pole with which to pummel the clothes while we yelled our heads off. One day, while we were belting away, Mr. Hill came in and the singing finished in mid-air. "If I had wanted to employ a set of choirboys, that's what I would have bloody employed," he shouted. "Now, get on with it!" but we didn't take any notice.

Although we were great friends, the Dye Shop was a "closed shop" in the sense that it was difficult to learn the secrets of the trade. Bert had been to Manchester for a special six week course on dyeing, and Charly was great - with delicate fabrics and delicate colours he was brilliant, but reluctant to share his knowledge. They went to the Dye Shed and mixed a bit of this and a bit of that, and a bit of the other, came back and mixed it into the boiling water, and then flicked it to create a skin of colour on the water.

In the end, Mr. Hill took me in hand, and said, "You will be the dyer of blacks and navy blues." He showed me how to mix the colours for black, all the different shades of black, and the same for navy blue. Bert and I became such buddies that he also shared a few secrets with me, and taught me how to look across the cloth to see its true colour.

Our duties extended to many different things. When the winter came and the work dropped off we weren't sacked. We had to decorate the factory, and help install equipment in the Speedy Laundry which was being built next door. We enjoyed this because we enjoyed working together - there was a "all for one and one for all" atmosphere, rather like a family atmosphere in the place, and we used to do good turns for each other. For example, one dodge was to come to work in our best clothes, change for work, and during the day put our best clothes through the cleaning process - then go home all poshed up. Nelly Johnson, who was an expert on the pleating machine, blocked me a trilby hat into a fashionable pork-pie hat - and that's how we looked after each other.

Most of the time you did thing simply because you were told to. Once I carried a bottle full of Spirits of Salt back to the factory on my lap in the firm's van. The driver, known as Speedy, took great care and there was no problem, but looking back on it, I realise I could have burned to death if the acid had spilled. Another time Mr. Evans fell while whitewashing some windows on the roof. His blood mixed with the whitewash he had prepared and Mr. Hill ordered me to the roof to carry on "pinkwashing"!

I later worked in the Press Shop and learnt to iron and work the Hoffman Presses, so I did learn many aspects of the business but about 1932 I left because the water was affecting my hands. Mr. Hill had left to start another business in Wolverhampton, and Mrs. Hill begged me to stay, but my father had found me a job at the Metropolitan Cammell works at Saltley. I realised my first love was engineering.

Years later I met Charly Harris at Handsworth Station one night and we travelled back to Blackheath together on the train. I haven't seen him again from that day to this, but on that journey all the past came together and I realised how thrilling those years had been at Valeting Services. It had been hard, but it had been a wonderful education.?

Above: Les Clough plays cards with a pack produced by Wolverhampton Steam Laundry as a "promotional item". (The laundry also gave away pencils, rulers, clothes brushes, and measuring tapes bearing the company's name.) The picture on the back of these cards is reproduced on the previous page, and Les himself is the fourth driver from the right. The entire fleet is lined up, and the vans working on the "Economy Wash" can be identified by their light boxes above the driver's cab. (WSL Collection)

Wolverhampton Steam Laundry

Les Clough

I started work at the Wolverhampton Steam Laundry in November 1927. I was appointed to a van driving job, so I was not too pleased to find myself working with a horse and delivery van for the first few months while I learnt the job. The laundry still had four horses, but was beginning to build up a fleet of vans. I was used to horses because my father had a horse and cart for his green grocery business in Wednesfield but I was keen to start driving. In 1928 they introduced the Economy Wash service and they wanted drivers for the expansion of the new service. I was given one driving lesson in a two gear Ford, and one lesson in the new three gear Morris. Each lesson consisted of one trip encircling West Park, and that was the extent of my training.

At the age of eighteen I became a driver, and each driver usually had one or two boys working with him - the boys being fourteen-year-olds straight from school. On Mondays it was quite common to have to collect up to five hundred parcels before two o'clock. We offered a Monday to Thursday service, a Tuesday to Friday service and a Wednesday to Saturday service. These alternated with a lighter a Thursday to Monday service and a Friday to Tuesday service, so the two smaller deliveries could be made after you had made the big morning collections.

We were not paid by the hour - we were paid for doing the job. The directors were adamant that deliveries came first, and that a journey could never be missed. Therefore, we started work at 7.00.am but there was no finishing time - a driver finished when he had completed his journey. The first hour of each day was spent unloading and re-loading the van, and then there was a break from eight until half past. Then we "paid in" the money received the previous day, and prepared to be on the road by nine o'clock. We might take half an hour for lunch but more likely we would eat our sandwiches as we drove along. Sometimes a journey was not completed until eight o' clock at night, and once or twice I did not finish until eleven. Whatever time we finished we had to return the van to the laundry, cash-up, and then take our receipt-book home to balance-up at night before going to bed - and be ready for work next morning at seven. Drivers took the money home with them as it was considered safer to disperse the day's takings overnight in this way.

After five year's driving I was taken off the road and put in charge of the van-men. This followed the arrival of a salesman from London. He took us out in small groups on canvassing exercises. I must have shown some talent because he suggested that I be put in charge of putting the men through salesmanship courses, so I became Under Sales Manager.

I controlled all the vehicles and all their comings and goings. The service had developed and expanded and we eventually had twenty four vans - twenty one for Wolverhampton Steam Laundry and three for The Sunshine Laundry. All the drivers had to come to me to see if there were any orders or enquiries that had come in by phone. I also had to make out a sheet to record their canvassing calls and follow-ups. Their canvassing was on top of their collecting and delivering work, and they received a bonus for new customers. A vehicle might carry five hundred parcels, so the parcels themselves occupied a lot of space and loading had to be carefully supervised. If a parcel was missing I would have to make enquiries in the packing department, and sort things out before the driver could depart.

It was a problem to keep all the vehicles properly manned. I needed a driver or boy who knew the round to each vehicle, and had to cover all absences. I had to go round with a list and check everybody off as I saw them - and I couldn't really breathe again until I knew I had all the teams I needed for the day's work. I also appointed new drivers and boys. There was quite a turnover of staff, and, just occasionally somebody had to be sacked. I used to support my drivers, and had to see that they did the job correctly, but I tried to be fair with everybody and I think it was appreciated. They would do anything for me because they knew I would back them in any dispute where they needed backing. Mr. Ryan, the Sales Manager, advised me against looking after the men too well!

Everybody had to be well turned-out in a uniform: a peaked cap and a uniform coat that was regularly cleaned. Each morning everyone had to report to me

for a clean Van Heusen collar in order to be turned out as a clean respectable laundry salesman. Mirrors had to be put up so that drivers could check that their collars and ties were worn correctly. The vans were kept very smart as well. On Wednesdays there was only a collection, there were no deliveries, so that was the day that drivers washed their van down. Drivers also had to clean the engine, back axle, gearbox and everything else, inside and out.

The vans were red, with a white roof and white lettering, beautifully coach-painted by Edwards of Lower Stafford Street. The Economy Wash vehicles had a neon lighting system on the front of the roof, and boards on the side saying, "Let the laundry do it all." We were recognised as a very smart outfit, and we used to mount advertising campaigns in which our vehicles would form a cavalcade and parade through the town. It was quite a show, and splashed Wolverhampton Steam Laundry on everybody's mind. In the days of Wolverhampton Hospital Carnival, we would dress up our vans for the show.

With tewnty four vans our garage stretched from Sweetman Street to Newhampton Road, and they were all packed in tightly. They all had to be kept on the road all the time, so we had our own fitting staff of two mechanics, who just had room to work on one vehicle at a time - but it meant we could do our own repairs.

Before the War I still went out almost daily to carry on with the canvassing work, and, on rare occasions, had to follow-up complaints. This ceased when the War began as I was made Transport Manager. It was required at the time that all fleets had a manager, but really my job was virtually unchanged. We loaned a few vans to the Wolverhampton Ambulance Service during the War, and, as I was involved in ambulance work, we carried out a few Wartime exercises. We also found new work: for example we collected laundry from RAF Cosford, from the time that comstruction of the camp began.

In the early sixties a new Sales Manager arrived, and revised all the journeys I had carefully worked out. He did not stay long, and after he had gone I was allowed to put everything back to how it was before, and was told that my new title was "Despatch Manager". So, I had three different job titles, but my job always really remained the same!

Nearly five hundred people were working for the laundry at that time, including about sixty five on the vans. It was a very sociable place and every Christmas we would have a really good party, and we often held dances and whist drives in the canteen. As there were so many girls employed by the company there was a shortage of men at the dances, so we invited the men from the ECC to provide partners for our girls. Many laundry staff married each other, and I suppose some of our girls married the chaps from the ECC. Many of the girls lived in Whitmore Reans, so it was "out-of-bed and into-work" for most of them, and we were a major employer in the area.

The company was started by Major Carr in 1890, later joined by Mr. Brockbank. Major Carr's son, Roger, was a popular director of the company, and similarly Mr.Brockbank's sons entered the business. Ted was on the administrative side, and his brother, Bowman, provided the laundry with his engineering expertise, so it was quite a family firm until everybody grew old. Although we enjoyed a monopoly in Wolverhampton the firm spent a great deal on advertising and loved to give out all sorts of gimmicks like pens, pencils, brushes, rulers and playing cards - all bearing the company name.

We were also proud of our testimonials from satisfied customers, like the stars who appeared at the town's theatres, and once we had Royal customers. When the Duke of Kent and Princess Marina honeymooned at Himley Hall we laundered the crested table linen, including the biggest table cloth I had ever seen: it must have been about fifty feet long. It was quite a problem to fold it correctly, and I don't know what we charged for it!

At one time everyone you met in town had worked at the Laundry, did work at the Laundry, or would like to work at the Laundry! If you worked at "The Bubble", you were one of the fortunate ones.

Wolverhampton Steam Laundry

Ena Walden

At the ripe old age of fourteen and a half I had taken a shorthand typing course and was all prepared for work in an office. However, it was difficult to obtain a job, and a friend continually urged me to apply to the company that she worked for: the Wolverhampton Steam Laundry. I went to see the Manageress, and she asked me to start the following Monday - in late February 1937.

My career started in the Sorting Room, checking in the work, working with the Supervisor and learning the job as I went along. It was interesting and I quite liked it, and liked the people I was working with. I spent three years there until a new Senior Supervisor arrived, and I was asked to go into the Packing Room. I had not been there very long when there was another change. A new manageress, Mrs. Blythe, came to the Wolverhampton Steam from the Watford Laundry, and I was moved back to the Sorting Room.
I was a Supervisor, and barely eighteen, but I made a job of it, and stayed for about two years.

This led to a promotion which led me back to the Packing Room. It was regarded as promotion because I was in charge of both racking and packing, but really the responsibility was no more than in the Sorting Room. If anything the supervision of the sorting was more important because it was the key to the whole process. If everything was sorted and marked correctly there was a fair chance that the garments would eventually return to the customer correctly. The eighteen month's training in supervising the packing was more pleasant than sorting simply because it involved handling the work when it was clean.

All my experience was being gained in what was called the Economy Wash, which the company provided as a cheaper alternative to its Fully Finished Service. The latter was carried out in a bay on the far side of the van shed, and to those of us on the Economy Wash the Fully Finished looked a very unattractive proposition. Perhaps it seemed uninviting because their work was so special and was handled as such - you couldn't get away with dropping anything on the floor in that service! Older and more experienced workers were employed on the Fully Finished Service, and the Assistant Manageress over there had a reputation for not getting on with young people.

There was one particular honour that we enjoyed on the Economy Service - we were the smaller part of the company's trade and therefore we worked shorter hours. When we left at four thirty or five o'clock they often carried on until six or seven. Better still, on Fridays, when we finished at half past twelve, they carried on until five. And the greatest joy of all was that we had to walk through their service to be paid on Friday, while they were still working.

When I was twentyone there was another management change, Mrs.Blythe went back to Watford, and Mrs.Dove came from Watford to Wolverhampton - they changed places. I worked for Mrs.Dove for the next sixteen years. She was very strict, in a Victorian style, but she was very good at her job, and was an excellent teacher. In the end, I felt I owed nearly all my knowledge of the laundry and its organisation to Mrs.Dove. She was a wonderful organiser.

Mrs.Dove transferred me to the Fully Finished Service, and I can still remember my response: "Oh No! Not into the Prison!" Once I worked there I realised how good it was, but that was my initial reaction to having to leave the younger, more light-hearted, atmosphere of the Economy Service in its newer brighter building. The Fully Finished was in an old windowless building where you didn't know it was raining until you came out of work at night and saw that it was wet. I had to be persuaded to go - but persuaded I was!

I had to start training all over again, and it was back to sorting, but this time sorting as practised by the Fully Finished Service. The work was different and the people seemed different simply because they were older. When I was in my twenties people who were over forty seemed so old. The oldest employee to retire from the Steam Laundry worked in the Wash House until she was eighty four.

Packing was also different, and there were new things to learn. Stiff collars had to go into curling bands to be packed, and semi-stiff collars had their own kind of band. Shirts were packed in bags that slipped everywhere. In the Economy Service we had packed the customer's laundry in paper, but now I had to learn to uses boxes and hampers. The Laundry supplied these and they had to be transferred from the sorters to the packers. It was all very complicated and time consuming, but the packing was of very high quality, and our well-made fibre boxes lasted for years. At first even handling the work was frightening - it wasn't just plonked in the box! However my training was such that I had to learn to do every job. It wasn't just a theoretical training.

Eventually the day came when I had to leave packing and go into the process rooms for the first time. (At one time the sections of the laundry were called "rooms", later we called them "departments", just as the terms, "forewoman", "chargehand" and "supervisor" were changed over the years). I found myself in the Calendar Room, where the work was very exacting. There was a lot more to concentrate on, running a whole sequence of operations on different machines: sheets on one machine, table cloths on another, and tray cloths and serviettes on another, handkerchiefs on yet another and towels going through tumblers. To master all these I would have to use my hands more than my head, at the same time as dealing with twice as many staff.

A chargehand or supervisor had to be working alongside people, or showing new people how to do the work; you could never sit back and simply "take charge", you had to be in the midst of everything. When the original chargehand from the Calendar Room retired we found it very difficult to replace her because so many people found it an unattractive job, but I must say that I found it very interesting, and I really enjoyed working in that room once I had the satisfaction of mastering all the processes. In fact it gave me a new confidence.

The table linen machines had different padding to the four-roller machines used for the sheets, and we prided ourselves on producing a good tablecloth. The machine gave the starched linen a very shiny look when polished, and it was important to learn when the machine needed re-clothing, and later, as we

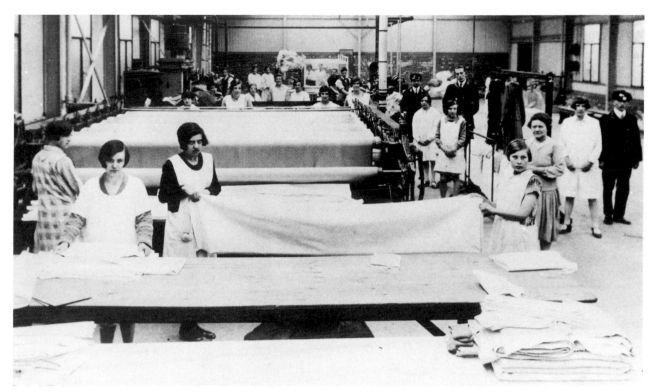

Above: The Econowash Department at Wolverhampton Steam Laundry in 1929. Mrs.Rogers, who was the manageress of the department at that time, is third from the right. Drivers Lol James, Horace Holloway and Walter Brown can be seen, and the girl, third from the left, has been identified as Winnie Freeman. Identification of folks in a sixty year old picture is possible because everyone worked at the laundry for such long periods of time!
(WSL Collection)

changed the machines, it was important to master each one to produce the same finish. When I felt I had mastered feeding the machine with a tablecloth, and then folding it as it came off, I felt I was getting somewhere in the laundry industry. Years later, when I was in management, I could still go along and produce a good tablecloth when something special was required.

One problem that I encountered was that the ladies had their own jargon when talking about the machines. If the sheet machine was a four-roller I would call it that, but they would call it "Nellie" or "Phyllis" or "The Horror". I could not bring myself to tell someone to, "Take that to Nellie," and I know Mrs.Dove would not have tolerated me saying, "We have had so many sheets per hour off Phyllis this morning." My job was to persuade everybody to call a machine by its correct name.

After only six months in the Calendar Room, I was moved to the Press Room, and once again there seemed to be so many difficult jobs to learn. The ladies in this room seemed particularly old - in their sixties and seventies. I seemed to be moving on all the time, so it seemed incredible to me to be able to look at a row of twelve ladies in their seventies who had been hand-ironing all their lives since the age of thirteen.

Hand presses were used to press coats, overalls, and chair and settee covers, and hand ironing was used as a "topping up" process. In the Press Room there was also an Airing Room, where anything that was

hand-ironed throughout had to be aired before it could be folded. I was working with a young chargehand who was full of life - we found we could get on with each other very well, and her name was Flossie Beckett. The Airing Room was very important to us - when we occasionally found five minutes respite from the work we could go there to discuss what had happened the previous night. Before I met Flossie I can truthfully say that I had never indulged in much conversation with anyone, other than about work. We had many laughs together, and I felt I was relaxing for the first time. I became more lighthearted about the job, and that enabled me to enjoy the work itself more - and perhaps that was why I was able to stay there so long.

After the Press Room, came the Shirt Department, where five units of three people processed about ten thousand shirts per week. To press a shirt was not an easy thing to learn - and it had to be "spot on". Even then all the shirts were topped up by hand ironing, and that is why it was an expensive service. (8d per shirt compared with 3d per shirt in the Economy Service.) Collars received special attention, and the lady who did them had been doing it for forty years and was a real master of her craft. Her name was Ady Bradley. The collar machines were very intricate and they blocked the starch into the collars, which then passed to the curling machines. Our visitors could never tear themselves away from the collar machines - they were so fascinating.

I also had to spend some time in the Wash House, seeing how the laundry was weighed and loaded into the machines. The work that came out of the machines was not spin-dried like today's washing. It came out wringing wet and had to be loaded onto barrows. This was heavy work and was done by men wearing rubber aprons. There were a few women working in the Wash House. For example there were a few on collar-starch-ing and some on scrubbing. The former made up their own starch in the dip - using different starches for each kind of collar, stiff, semi-stiff and wing collars.

Shirts were very soiled when they came to the Laundry from people who worked in factories. We would not have got them clean in the washing machines, so the ladies scrubbed them. Two old ladies scrubbed all day from eight until seven. They seemed to love it, and they worked until retiring age. In fact, everybody at the Laundry seemed to live to a great age so it didn't do us any harm! From the Wash House the wet washing was taken to the Hydro for a four-minute spin. If the Hydro was not balanced it made a tremendous clatter and everybody knew about it. Once the garments were well spun they were taking to the Calendar Room, where my practical training had begun.

It took two and a half years to make my way through all this training, and I felt ready for the promotion by the time I became Senior Supervisor. It was a big leap in responsibility but not financially. Laundries could never afford to pay large wages because they had such big staffs - in my care alone, there were one hundred and eighty people at one stage. Our wages were in line with shop assistants and hairdressers - the lowest paid! Although I felt that I would never be able to paint the town red, I was glad to have regular work, and to be doing something that I enjoyed.

The laundry job itself was always demanding, and often there was no let-up. I was frequently tempted to forego my teabreaks just to keep abreast of everything, but the pleasant side of it all was meeting and working with the Flossie Hacketts of the business. As I shall explain in a moment, the side of the work that involved working with people got better and better as time went on.

In 1962 there was another change in management when Mrs.Dove retired. Peter Thurley came to the laundry, and introduced a breath of fresh air into the place, having just completed eighteen months as a Time and Motion consultant to the company. He introduced a bonus scheme, and started the move towards using less labour. The Brockbanks, who owned the laundry, were very fair with the workforce. Although they gave Mr.Thurley the job of getting the job done faster and more efficiently with less staff, they did not expect him to go about this by sacking people. As people retired or left they were not replaced, and over the next twenty five years the number of staff employed fell from about two hundred and fifty to about seventy. In the process rooms the staff fell from about one hundred and eighty to about thirty.

I was promoted to Production Manager as Mr.Thurley moved on to become General Manager, and my final position was that of Works Manager. When I was fifty six I remember saying to the boss, "You do realise that I only have four more years until retirement". The tradition of long service at the laundry lingered on, as he replied, "Come and see me again when you are seventy - we'll talk about it then."

As it happened, I didn't feel ready for retirement at sixty. I simply did not want to leave, but I did feel it would be a good idea to fix a date for retirement otherwise I might have found myself going on forever and not have the chance to enjoy retirement. I decided to leave at the age of sixty five, but, in the event, I did stay one year longer than that.

The interesting thing is that I enjoyed the second half of my career at the laundry more than the first half. In my early career I had enjoyed learning all the jobs and becoming more confident, but what was really satisfying was that during the second twenty five years I could set about creating a happier, lighter, working environment. This is what I had first encountered in the Economy Wash, but it all became so serious in the Fully Finished Service and the regime was so strict. As I grew older I loved to take on young people, and I loved working with them. I think we managed to create a happy atmosphere in which to work - I certainly enjoyed it tremendously.

Left: Hop pickers from Tipton at Stiffords Bridge in the 1920's. On the extreme right are Elizabeth McCann and Louis Whitehouse, known as the "Wall Sisters". (Ann Thomas' Collection)

5

HOP PICKING

On the last page of "Black Country Folk at Werk" is a photograph of hop pickers at Tenbury Wells which has prompted a number of people to volunteer information and memories relating to this kind of work for inclusion in this book. In the left foreground of that picture is Elsie Briscoe with her daughter, Edna, on her knee. Edna herself continues the story here, and in this picture Edna can be seen with her mother, Elsie, on the left, and her son, Jack, in her arms. On the right is Edna's sister, Betty Briscoe, holding Edna's daughter, Anita. They were photographed at Shelsley Beauchamp about 1950.

The full story of hop growing (not just "picking") can be found in "A Pocketful of Hops", published by the Bromyard Historical Society in 1988, with many contributions from Black Country folk.

Hop Picking

Edna Smart (nee Briscoe)

In the photograph at the back of *Black Country Folk at Werk* I can be seen as a young girl sitting on my mother's knee among the hop pickers at Depper's Farm, Tenbury Wells, about 1924. Hop picking was part of my Mother's way of life, and, in turn, it became part of my life. By 1950 I was able to take my children to the hop fields, but now that way of life has gone.

Although we had worked near Tenbury, I have better memories of working on Moore's Farm near Shelsley Beauchamp. Every year the farm used to send word to Mom, and the folk in Wednesbury used to come to her to say that they wanted to go. About fifty of us went from Wednesbury. At first they used to fetch we on lorries, but later they sent coaches, and the lorries took our trunks and tin boxes. Although no men were allowed when we went fruit picking near Bromsgrove, a few men and youths did come along to the hop picking. Really they would have anybody provided you were of good character.

We lived in chalets arranaged one room per family back to back, and some folks lived in the barns. We slept on straw beds but the accommodation was all right. We lived in our wellingtons and the folks who came down to see us at the wekends probably thought we were really scruffs, but as far as I was concerned it was great. There have been times when we were up to our knees in sludge, but I can only remember the times when the sun was shining!

The Moores were good bosses to work for - not like some owners who could behave like old squires and thought nothing of putting a whip across your back.

Sometimes my Mother went hop tying earlier in the year, then we would go fruit picking in June and July, and then the hop picking - so we were away all summer, we were never at school. If there were any disputes my Mother was the spokesperson who would have to sort it out - for example, if people weren't satisfied with what they were getting for the hops. We never picked hops on a Sunday, and fruit was not picked on Saturday because there was no market the next day.

There was many a time we put our Jack in the bottom of the crib, and we would be picking and picking while he slept, and we would find him covered in hops, maybe just the top of his head showing! And, of course, there were good days and bad days. The best hops, the "fuggles" were bigger, and it didn't take so many to make a bushel: three bushel for 1/3d. But sometimes the hops were small and blighted with black fly, you couldn't make money with them, and you would be covered in black fly. If the weather was too hot the hops used to powder up, leaving you with a handful of petals. The black powder on the insides of the hops got on your hands, and it was very bitter, so, if you stopped to eat a sandwich you had to wrap it in paper to hold it.

Mobile shops came round, and the Sally Army came every day and provided first aid, and tea and cakes for a penny. For a penny a pint you could have fresh milk that was still warm. We had our main meal at the end of the day, and it always seemed to grow dark early. Everybody was in bed by nine o'clock, and we soon fell asleep after telling ghost stories. We were up again by 5.30. or 6.00.am.

Years ago we used to meet the Gypsies, but they didn't seem to come so much in later years, not the real Gypsies, but we did see some travellers. They always seemed so happy in their way of life, and we were happy on the farm. They were as good as gold, but if any of our men so much as looked at their women, the knives were out! I did see one or two fights between Black Country folk and the Gypsies.

On Sundays we would go for strolls. My sister and I took the kids while my Mother stayed round the fire making Sunday dinner. We tramped for miles, or went to see the hill-climbs at Shelsley. All sorts of famous people came down for those hill-climbs. Once I saw Jean Harlow or someone like that, in a small plane, landing in the meadow. If there was nothing else to do we could always go scrumping.

It was a very free life, and we worked with everybody around us so there were always plenty of laughs and jokes. For my mother it was a way of life, but for us it was more like a holiday. If you came back with £6 you were well off - you were rich.

Below: Bob Hosier, who has described his experience as a photographer at Dudley's Hippodrome (Page 14), was invited to join the Midlands Branch of the Brewers Guild on its annual inspection of the hop fields, about 1948. He took this photograph of the pickers from the Dudley area somewhere in the Teme Valley on the Worcester/Herefordshire border. At the back of the group we can see the corrugated iron "barracks" in which the pickers lived. (Bob Hosier)

Hop Picking

Sylvia Shaw (nee Tibbetts)

For the first ten years of my life I was taken hop-picking every September, by my Mother. Every time my Mom went she seemed to have a new baby to bring along, and as my sisters grew older they stayed at home with my Dad, who was a chain-maker. It was the only holiday we ever had but Mom didn't take us along just to play about - we had to work hard, and, as a family, we needed the money. As we grew up we helped Mom, and we seemed to know how to do the work instinctively, even if our first trip to the hop yard was in a pram, with the wheels all clogged-up with clay!

As the time approached each year, Mom would say, "I'm not going this year," and we would have to pester her to go. Perhaps she only said it to tease us. The farm recruited hop-pickers through Mrs.Stafford, their agent in Quarry Bank, and it was rumoured that the connection was first established when one of the hop-growers had married a woman from Quarry Bank. If we wanted to go we had to go and tell Mrs.Stafford, and later we were told the date of departure and the time we would be picked up. Really the party consisted of much the same people from year to year.

At the appointed time we assembled at Merry Hill, taking our hop picking boxes down there on a barrow, or on prams. Our luggage included seats, stools and umbrellas and everything we would need. Sometimes the luggage had to be taken to the farm in a lorry. We boarded a coach operated by Yarrington's, sent from the farm to collect us. Off we went to Cooper's Farm, near Knighton-on-Teme.

There was a certain barrack that my Mom liked, where we could have our own fire. The barracks were wooden sheds that were cleaned and limed before we arrived. They were good buildings, and still looked quite good when they were burned down many years later. There was also a brick building which was roofed, but had an open front. This was known as the "Shanty", and when it rained fires were lit beneath special chimneys, and the cooking and baking could continue. There were tables and trestles for people to put out their breakfasts. The shanty has been made into a proper house now.

One year, as we arrived at our barrack, Mom lifted a mat, and there we found a new-laid egg, so we had egg for tea! Soon after arriving we had to sort out our beds - a rectangle of straw, held in place by logs. Some folks slept in the cow sheds, and one fellow, who still lives in Quarry Bank today, slept right next door to the bull.

Mr.Stafford used to light the fires, and these fires were quite massive, because everybody had to boil water, cook, prepare breakfasts and everything. We children had to fetch the water from the pumps. Really it was quite awkward to provide meals, but Mom would always cook, and on some days she took a kettle with her and lit a fire in the hop yard. We ate lots of tinned corn beef, and salmon paste and jam! It was

Below: Annie Tibbetts, from Quarry Bank, with her daughter Sylvia, by a hop pickers' crib, about 1950.

like camping really, but it wasn't too primitive. Our tasks included leaving the tilly lamps for Coopers to fill each morning, and we had to collect them as we returned from the fields, and we also bought our bread and milk from the Coopers. Occasionally we could pick up mail from the farmhouse.

The first day of going down to the hop yard we all had to collect our cribs. Every year Mom put a bow, a ribbon from the hair of one of her children, onto the crib so that we should know which one to pick next year. Just our family worked around our crib, but some people picked on their own and shared a crib by partitioning it. We were proud that our family was noted for being good pickers.

There were three pole-pullers, two men from Quarry Bank, and one local man who owned a small-holding. They pulled the vines down off the wires. We had to pull the branches off the vine, and then there was a certain way of holding each one, holding the leaves back, so that you could rip the hops off. I did it left-handed even although I was normally right-handed. So many vines were called a house, and some parts of the hop yard were better for working in than others. Nobody liked to be on the end of the hop yard because the vines were very thin and the hops were very small, so those vines were pulled down and shared out among the pickers so that there was no quarrelling.

When the picking stopped and it was time to bushel, they used to shout, "Pick 'em up and clear 'em out." We had to pick the hops up off the floor, and clear the leaves out of the crib. If there were too many leaves left they would not bushel, but we were always clean pickers! We would leave Mom in the hop yard to get bushelled and we would go off to start the fire going and to fetch water. Our hands were usually stained by the work, but we used some groundsel (chickweed) that could be rubbed on your hands to remove the stain. It left your hands smelling horribly, but it took the stains out.

One year we went on strike. We found that another place was getting more money than us. Perhaps we were getting 10d when they were geting 11d - but our strike was successful, and we were then paid the higher rate. The last year we went, when I was eleven, Dad came with us. While he was chain-making a cinder had fallen into his boot and his foot was ulcerated. The doctor said it would do him good to come with us. That year we went home with £100 - such a lot of money - but I don't know what my mother did with it!

In the evening, after the meal, it was possible to have a pint of cider - if you wanted it you went to the kilns and they gave it to you. Some evenings, after the children were asleep, some of the women went to the pub for a drink. On Sunday mornings we were visted by the Hop Pickers Mission, and to the accompaniment of a piano accordian we used to sing hymns like, "What a Friend we have in Jesus". One year the ministers, Mr. Luton and Mr. Lemon, came to Quarry Bank. They found my mother out and took her up to the Community Centre where she was given a Bible.

There were other visitors - the rabbit man came round once a week, and we used to stew the rabbits. Even the Italian ice cream man from Quarry Bank came all the way out to see us so that we could buy his ice cream! Sister Christine, a Sister of Mercy, came to the farm every day to provide First Aid. She came with a priest in a car, but where they came from I do not know. She seemed to favour our family, and we thought she was very kind. We all had coughs all the time because we loved her cough medicine. Wasp stings were very common, and she treated these with blue stuff - gentian violet.

On Saturdays we finished at dinnertime and had the afternoon off, and this was a time for visitors to come to the farm. Dad used to arrive with a big blue suitcase full of goodies - like chocolates provided by my sisters who worked at Cadbury's, or big pies that they had baked for us at home. He came all the way by bus, and all the visitors had to leave at the same time to catch the one bus back home.

We enjoyed life on the farm. We used to go mushroom picking, and we used to help drive the cows in. There were wonderful orchards nearby and we learnt the varieties of apple. Scrumping did take place occasionally. but it was said that the farmers were watching with binoculars! Justice was administered on the spot, and, on one occasion a lad was birched for breaking a plum tree. His parents said nothing because they knew their son was in the wrong. We used to look for caterpillars in the hops: one was green and one had a pink fur on it, which we called the "hop cat". We used to keep them in match boxes! We lived in Wellingtons - and I've hated them ever since.

The season usually began a few days before we were due to return to school, and thus we missed at least three weeks schooling at the beginning of each new school year. When you returned to school, you were called out and given a roasting, but we had to be thick-skinned about it. When I started my secondary school they threatened to prosecute if we were kept away from school and that was the last year that I went - about 1950.

They were wonderful summers, even though it rained non-stop once and some of the fields were flooded. Our first treat on returning to Quarry Bank each autumn was a visit to the pictures - to the Coronet, where they said you could see the mice running up the curtains.

Hop Picking Memories

Ethel Barlow

My Mother, My Aunt, and myself went hop picking to Tenbury Wells, from 1923 to 1928. I can remember that we had to walk from Church Hill, Wednesbury, where we lived, to a house in Witton Lane, Hill Top. A woman, named Mrs. Pope, lived there, and she gave us the train tickets (one-way only) to enable us to reach the Hop Yards at Tenbury Wells.

It was always on 1st September, and was supposed to be for one month, but sometimes it was longer, depending on the weather. I was kept away from school to join my Mother hop picking, but after 1928 I could not go again because the Education Authorities threatened to prosecute!

When we arrived at the farm we were put in cow sheds that had been cleaned out and white-washed - with a corner for each family. We had straw for the beds, and a sack filled with straw for a pillow. Most people took a large tin chest, which served as a table, and the lighting in the cow sheds came from paraffin hurricane lamps

Each morning we were taken to the hop fields in farm wagons, and stayed in the fields until four o'clock. The men were called pole-pullers. They cut the hops down to take to the women who stripped the hops into the cribs. At the end of each day the men would leave first to go and catch rabbits from the fields, and these could be eaten with the potatoes with which we were supplied. A large communal fire was set up outside the cow sheds, and a nourishing meal could usually be cooked for everyone. There were blackened tin kettles all round the fire. The tea was always smoke dried, and tasted awful, but one got used to it.

One year it rained continually for the whole of the month, so picking hops was out of the question as they were no good when picked wet. If you did not work, you did not get paid. The year it rained we almost starved, but my Aunt took me with her to a lot of the large houses in Tenbury Wells in order to beg. One family gave us a meal, another gave us jam, sugar, and bread, and another family rigged me out - me, a little girl, rigged out in a boy's sailor suit! I was too young to care then, but now I have to smile when I think about it. The reefer coat had brass anchor buttons, and my hat had "HMS Victory" on the hat band. With me in my boots, I must have looked ridiculous.

When we were paid it was only a pittance, anyway. We earned three, or sometimes four, pence a bushel, and it took a lot of hops to make a bushel. As most of the pickers were subbed at the end of the day, they had no wages to come at the end of the week. But some years it was not too bad - when we had good weather.

The women used to keep the very young children in the cribs while they were working, and the kiddies loved it. The busheller, as he was called, although he was called other names by some of the women, came to the cribs four times a day with his basket and farm cart. He used to press down hard on the basket to get as many in as he could, and as they were so light it took a lot of hops to make a bushel. A lot depended on the size of the hops - some years they were very large, some years they were very small. At the end of a day we, and the other families, would find we had only earned a shilling.

The highlight of the day was when the milkman arrived in his pony and trap, and the bread man would come round the fields about noon. Bread and milk never tasted so delicious, at the time, or since that time.

It was a five-day week, and on Saturday and Sunday we could have walks around the town or down the country lanes. The Salvation Army always came to the farm on Sunday with a brass band. They always enjoyed a large audience who joined the community singing. On Sunday mornings we used to stand outside the Swan Hotel to watch the Meet. The men in their red coats looked very grand with their horses and hounds. The men had glasses of port, and the hounds were raring to go, but I was too young at that time to realise what it all meant. No way would I watch a spectacle like that again - my sympathy lies with the fox.

My family had to go hop picking every year, because if they had refused there would be no labour money. As I had no father, we had no option. Every year I was allowed a pair of boots out of the Poor Children's Boot Fund in Wednesbury. They were boys' lace-ups, with steel tips on the toes and heels, and came in very useful in the muddy fields of the hop yards. We returned home in a very raggle taggle state - and all the family seemed to have for our labours was a sack of apples, a spray of hops, and very little money.

The Walsall Hop-Pickers

Walsall, like most other towns in the Black Country, witnessed the annual departure every September of numerous families making for the hop-fields. They disappeared into Herefordshire and Worcestershire for about three weeks and then came home to face proceedings for keeping the children from school. In 1934 the Walsall Observer sent a reporter along to describe what was going on, and the words that follow are a digest of his report.

The charming stretch of hop-country beyond Malvern is a veritable fairyland, invaded by the hop-pickers every year. To use their own words, these people "go down the country", and for many it is like an annual holiday, as well as an opportunity to earn a little extra money.

A strange stillness seemed to have settled over the landscape when I visited it this week on a day of golden sunshine. Only a few miles away were the dark masses of the Malvern Hills, and nearer at hand were the lesser hills, tree clad and verdant. Nestling beneath the hills were the hop fields, with their lines of poles and wires - the hops climbing in serried ranks up the strings, and fairly well laden. The dry season has not brought a bumper crop, but generally speaking the hops are a good size. Every now and then the stillness was broken by the hum of a tractor, or the animated laughter and chatter of the hundreds of pickers who were hidden behind the tall hedges and under the cover of the hop lines. They were not easy to discover.

This is the village of Suckley - a scattered village with no apparent centre. The parish church standing almost alone with no other companion than a prosperous farm, the station three and a half miles away, and the tavern at least a mile away in the other direction. All around, as far as you can see, are acres of hops and orchards. The farmsteads are well kept and tidy. Many of them bear the names of "Court" or "Grange". The place where the Walsall pickers are staying is called Winthill, and it is owned by an ex-Army Captain. "He's a real gentleman, he is," said one, "if we have any grouse and we go the proper way about it through the head woman and the bailif he generally has things put right."

Another picker told me about the work: "There's no art in hop-picking - its just a matter of putting your mind to the job. There's them that come and won't put their backs into it - and they are the first to grumble. They say its cold getting up first thing in the morning. The hops stain their fingers and they don't like that. Standing makes their legs ache and they wouldn't like to get wet for worlds. Oh, they make me tired. I've been coming here for years and never taken any harm yet."

"Some of them that stand rodneying at the street corners would be better employed if they came down here and did a bit of work," said the head woman, who engages the pickers for the farmer. It is the usual custom for the farmer to pay for the fare of the pickers there and back, and provide them with accommodation, blankets and firing. Sometimes they get tea and sugar, and maybe cider. The farmer also carts the belongings of the pickers, their tin boxes and the like, to and from the station. They buy most of their own food from vans which visit the hop-fields.

Standing at a picking "crib", a wooden contraption with sacking, into which the hops are placed, I found Mrs. Morris of John Street. she is sixty six years of age and has been going "down the country" for years. Then there was Mrs. Hodson, of Burrows Street, and members of her family, and others from the Ryecroft area. Mr. Corrington of 111 Beatrice Street, who is a cook in the 5th Battalion, South Staffordshire Regiment was busy picking, also Mr. William Ferber of Winson Green, who, with some pride said he was "one of Pat Collins' oldest hands. I used to work on his machines. He'll laugh when he knows I've come picking." There were tiny children in prams near the crib, and toddlers were playing "tick" around the hop-poles.

A man was going round with a hook on the end of a stick, and pulling the hops down ready for picking. He had the dignity of being "a pole man". The bailiff stood at hand with a watchful eye, ready to measure the hops into bushels and credit each picker with the amount due. I also talked with the nurse, sent by Worcester County Council, to watch the pickers' health.

"The trouble is that a lot of these children are not used to the open air," she told me. "They live in tiny houses where there are large fires. Down here it is very different. They are up early in the morning when the dew is rising. Then there is the fruit. They stuff themselves with fruit and make themselves ill."

One picker told me that, "The Education Committee people ought to be burnt. I've got a batch of six summonses waiting for me when I get back - all because I've brought the nippers here. What else can you do with them when you want to earn an honest penny? In Cradley Heath they have a holiday when the hopping is on. In Walsall they say we ought to have the holidays in August. I call it scandalous!"

I inspected the barracks where the pickers slept, and their fires where the cooking was done. A little girl was standing by a brazier cooking potatoes. "Mother's down the fields," she said, "and I stay here and look after the baby and my brother." Brother was gathering coke, and the tiny tot was peeping through a gate, watching pigs eating fallen apples in the orchard. Clothes were hung out to dry on barbed wire.

As I made my way back to the station, a wagon rumbled by laden with "pockets" of hops. They had been dried and sulphured in the kilns, and were bound for Worcester in preparation for the hop-fair. Most of the folks will be "hopping" for the next fortnight. Then back to Walsall, and the school summonses.

Left: Hop picking machine at work in the Teme Valley about 1948. Attempts to mechanise the hop picking process began in the 1930's. This is an example of the McConnel Hinds "flying finger" machine. After the War, Rubery Owen, of Darlaston, were responsible for installing these machines (see Jack Winship's story on page 43), but they were superceded by the more successful Bruff machines. Stripped bines can be seen returning to the ground on the right. By the mid 1960's hop picking by hand, with casual labour from places like the Black Country, had virtually ceased. (Bob Hosier)

6

LOCAL NEWS

County Express

Jack Haden

I recall one mid-April morning in 1934: I was working in the reporters' room, composing a paragraph about a local event. Suddenly a sturdy figure in a dark suit appeared in the doorway of the room occupied by the editor and sub-editor, of the County Express for North Worcestershire and South Staffordshire, to give our paper its full title. There he stood, quizzically surveying the scene.

He gazed at the partly exposed beams, whitewashed to match the ceiling and upper areas of the walls, the mottled yellowy wallpaper extending up some seven feet from the brown lino-covered floor. In the corners the paper was pealing from the roughly plastered walls. On one side of the room was a large window extending from almost the floor level to above the eaves into what must have been a dormer light. Against another wall was an old black-painted firegrate, occupied by a small gas fire, in front of which was a small rectangular metal tray containing half an inch of water and some soggy cigarette ends.

In the middle of the room was a long wooden table covered with oilcloth which had been carelessly slashed in a couple of places with a penknife. Four shabby chairs, one with a worn horse-hair upholstered seat, and two furnished with lumpy cushions, were stationed round the table, on which stood a telephone, a large dictionary, a pot of gum, a pair of scissors, sheets of copy-paper, and mutilated copies of recent editions of the paper. In one corner of the room, near the gas fire, stood a roll-topped desk, and an office armchair - its seat adorned with a rubber ring aircushion, for its occupant, the chief reporter, suffered from piles. The pigeon-holes of the desk were filled with a miscellany of booklets, diaries, pencils, clippings from newspapers, etc. The drawers of the desk contained the "cemetery" - rows of envelopes containing cuttings and notes on local people and events, arranged alphabetically. This was our reference library. Next to his desk was a shelf laden with County Council Reports and many years' accumulation of note books containing verbatim accounts of meetings he had attended. The only other piece of furniture was a cupboard which contained our store of reporters' note-books and copy-paper, and scrapbooks contain-

In the autumn of 1985 newspaper boys congregate outside Round's Newsagents, Blackhalve Lane, Wolverhampton. When the "Town Final" arrives at half past four the papers will be marked up and delivered to your door. The newspaper round is still the first encounter with paid work for many young people, and in this section we hear from two other folk who played a part in bringing you the news.

ing a record of the half-tone blocks that had been used over the years.

This was the scene that I had first encountered in the autumn of the previous year, and that now met the gaze of our unknown visitor. After looking around, all he said was, "How typical." Seconds later he was joined by the statuesque figure of a woman with a round, heavily made-up, face. Perhaps she was less familiar with provincial newspaper offices, but she made no comment. After glancing around she led her husband away.

A few minutes after their departure, we were informed by the editor that our visitors had been Caradoc Evans, an author and playwright, and his wife, a prolific writer of novels and plays, using the names Countess Barcynska and Oliver Sandys. Not surprisingly our editor had been impressed, and glad to give them his personal attention, for it was very unlikely that the County Express had ever before been visited by two people with entries in *Who's Who*. What could have induced them to penetrate the decrepit range of buildings in Victoria Passage, Stourbridge, other than to seek publicity for some enterprise?

It seemed that the lady had written a play called "Chappy - That's All", which was to be staged for three nights at the Scala Cinema, in Lower High Street. So impressed was our editor, Herbert Hadgkiss, that he wrote about the play and published a picture of the author. Kenneth Ewart Bolton, esteemed as the most "literary" of the reporting staff, was sent along on the first night to write a review. Unfortunately Ken Bolton was not impressed by the play, but such was the prestigious position of the paper's theatre critic, that he was allowed to express his personal opinion rather write an uncritical puff. Ken had been an older contemporary of mine at Stourbridge Grammar School, and he was one of several to be launched from the County Express into distinguished careers in journalism. I myself had the vaulting ambition to become the drama critic of The Times - but, alas, it was not to be.

From the "Literary" Sixth Form at the Grammar School, I joined the County Express as an indentured reporter in September 1933, at the age of seventeen. For the first twelve months my wage was ten shilings a week. While engaged in a telephone conversation about an advertisement with the paper's manager, my father mentioned that he had a son who had just left school. My father was invited to bring me along one evening to meet the editor, and while my father discussed football with the manager, I was questioned by Mr.Hadgkiss. Apart from my literary interests he seemed most impressed by the fact that I neither smoked nor drank. I later found out that he was a teetotal non-smoker and pillar of the Congregational Chapel, and that he had had unhappy experiences with reporters who imbibed too freely - an occupational hazard in journalism.

Having started my career, I found my abstemiousness was a handicap. Some people regarded it as eccentric and unsociable! It was often assumed that reporters were endowed with a great thirst, and when attending certain gatherings the host would almost immediately offer me a drink. Only a few weeks after starting I was entrusted with the reporting of the annual prize distribution of a domino or some such league at the Turk's Head at Audnam. No sooner had I found a seat and placed my pencil and notebook on the small table, than I was urged to have a drink. "Come on - have a whisky, it will make you write faster." The invitation repeatedly being refused, the host gave up and ordered a Vimto for me. I believe I reported the proceedings accurately.

In those 1930s days of unemployment, every Thursday afternoon I had to obtain the latest figures from Stourbridge Labour Exchange. Although the Black Country seemed to fare better that some other parts of industrial Britain there was, undoubtedly, some poverty and hardship. Nevertheless, people were amazingly cheerful and uncomplaining, as I discovered when calling at centres set up for the unemployed. There must have been some who had a lean time, but what astonished me, as I moved about the Black Country, was the enormous quantities of food and drink consumed, especially by working men.

On one occasion I attended the annual supper of a bowling or pigeon-flying club in Old Hill. As the assembled company of men from the chain shops, engineering works, foundries and brickyards were convivially engaged around the bar, the meal began about three quarters of an hour later than planned. Stewards appeared bearing large plates of roast mutton, on which were piled mounds of boiled potatoes, cauliflower and onions. I was still half way through my first generous helping by the time the others had completed their second, and then, to my surprise, came the second course, this time roast beef piled high with vegetables. After this came roast pork, and then large deep slices of apple pie and custard, then bread and cheese, celery and pickled onions. All the time jugs of beer were being emptied and refilled. I realised I was in danger of missing my bus home so I had to have a quick word with the secretary, jotting down the names of the prize winners, and made a discreet exit before the congratulatory speeches began. I felt replete without having sampled the beef, pork, or afters.

I would have found it difficult to imagine such scenes when I had arrived on my first day at the County Express. My mother had made sure that I was smartly turned out in a navy blue serge suit. I arrived at the main door well before nine o'clock, but there was no sign of life until the editor arrived at dead on nine. He led me through the dark narrow reception office and up a ramshackle wooden staircase, through an dusty anteroom, to his office. On his desk was the editorial typewriter and a telephone.

He then took me into the reporters' room, which I have already described, and I was introduced to the Chief Reporter, and then to the juniors as they arrived. The previous most junior reporter then took my journalistic training in hand, conducting me round the offices, and the printing works, indicating roughly how a newspaper was produced. I was shown the tasks that a junior was expected to do.

First I had to study copies of recent issues of the paper to familiarise myself with the paper's content and style. Then I was told how to preserve old half-tone blocks, used to print the pictures in the paper. They had to be smeared with grease, sealed in used envelopes, labelled and indexed, and filed away in cardboard boxes that lined shelves along a dark and dusty passage on the ground floor. On the second day, the Chief Reporter asked me to make a cup of tea. My spirit was willing, but being so inexperienced in domestic matters, the brew that I produced fell short of the standard required, so I was not asked to perform that service again. I was the sent to dust some two hundred bound copies of the paper that had not been disturbed for decades and were covered with dust,which was a task which I attacked with vigour. but my smart blue serge suit was soon thickly impregnated with grey dust.

Another tiresome job given to the junior reporter was to collect newsletters from Stourbridge Town Station and the Bus Depot. These newsletters were despatched by train or bus from our representatives in the outlying districts. We had one covering Rowley Regis and Halesowen, one covering Cradley and Cradley Heath, and another in Brierley Hill and Quarry Bank. They were dispatched at irregular intervals, the sender telephoning the editor to say they were on the way. The system worked well, unless the porter at Stourbridge Junction forgot to transfer our parcel to the branch-line train, and our newsletter would go on to Kidderminster and back to Birmingham! Sometimes a bus conductor would forget to hand in the parcel at Stourbridge Depot, and it would continue on its way up to Dudley. The junior reporter had to wait until the parcels turned up. Still it was a training in journalism: a profession fraught with frustration, wasted time and misunderstandings.

I graduated to reading the copy to correctors of proofs, and was eventually entrusted with "making the calls". This entailed telephoning outlying police stations each morning to see if anything untoward had occurred. Strict economy was exercised in running the County Express so calls to Stourbridge Police and Fire Stations were made on foot. This had the advantage of providing personal contact with the officers concerned - important in creating a happy relationship. Many small items of news were sent into the office in scrappy notes and it was the junior's job to rewrite such material.

Each Head Office reporter was allocated a district for which he was responsible, in terms of collecting details of what was taking place and maintaining contact with key people. The junior was made responsible for the Stourbridge district, which was the least demanding as so much material was dropped into the office regularly. Later I covered other districts, travelling by bus, by bike, or on foot. At one period I would visit Harts Hill and Holly Hall each Wednesday morning, and in the afternoon would cycle round Hagley, Clent, and West Hagley, calling on the clergy, and well-informed local people like schoolmasters, shopkeepers, and the clerk to the Parish Council. I could usually depend on obtaining a paragraph or two from the village blacksmith at Holy Cross. All the district paragraphs had to be on the editor's desk by 3.pm.

As a raw junior I was introduced to the reporting of more substantial events by accompanying a more experienced reporter to a few meetings and to the Magistrate's and County Courts. Within a few weeks I was out on my own, finding there were plenty of opportunities for error of omission and commission. People were sensitive about the spelling of their names, and it was easy to confuse a Vicar with a Rector, or a Borough Council with a Town Council. People had to be given their full initials and titles. Full and accurate reports were insisted upon. The selecting of just sensational statements, and writing up "stories" with disproportionate emphasis on certain aspects of the news, received little encouragement. Speeches were often quoted verbatim, and it was essential to take good shorthand notes.

There was a tendency to give flattering attention to public officials, business and professional people. It was accepted that, in general, people were vain, and that all but a few (those involved in court proceedings) welcomed a mention in the paper. It could be said that circulation figures of the County Express were based on names - columns and columns of them.

The County Express in the 1930s normally contained 24 broadsheet pages, and some weeks two or three pages were changed in the Rowley Regis and Halesowen edition. The editorial staff consisted of the Editor, a sub- editor, the Chief Reporter, and three junior reporters at Head Office, and three district reporters. One became a senior at the age of twentyfour, when the rate of pay, negotiated by the National Union of Journalists, was about £4.10s per week. From Monday to Friday one was on duty from nine till five with an hour for lunch, and from nine till noon on Saturday, but throughout the year I was occupied almost every Saturday afternoon, sometimes on Sundays, and on most Bank Holidays, and at least two evenings a week. As young reporters we frequently worked a sixty hour week. On one occasion I ventured to ask the Editor if I could have a Thursday afternoon off to attend a play in Birmingham. He was so taken aback that he agreed.

Many County Express reporters took advantage of the "training", and then moved on to daily journalism. Harold Evans went to the Sheffield Telegraph and after a distinguished career during the War, became Advisor on Press Relations to Prime Ministers Harold Macmillan and Sir Alec Douglas Home. Ken Bolton joined the Daily Mail, and eventually became Editor of the East African Standard. Arthur Norman Walker became Editor of the Midland Chronicle at West Bromwich and was later Night Editor of the Daily Mirror. Our district reporter in Cradley Heath before the War was John Clement Jones. From 1960 to 1971 he was Editor, and from 1971 to 1974 a Director, of the Express and Star. Some stayed at the County Express, and produced a provincial weekly that kept its public well informed and earned the respect of that public which tended to regard anything printed in the "County" as gospel truth. I was on the staff from September 1933 to September 1981, though absent on War Service for six years. For thirty years I was Chief Reporter.

Below: The composing room of the Express & Star, Queen Street, Wolverhampton, in the early 1930s. In the foreground compositors are setting headlines by hand, surrounded by Lino-type machine operators. (Express & Star)

Hot Metal

Albert Booth

I was fourteen when I started in the printing trade. I went to work at a place called the Church Press, in Lichfield Street, Wolverhampton, in Wheeler's Fold, between Baker's Shoe Shop and Cook's Travel Office. We did printing for churches throughout the country: church magazines, Easter and Christmas cards etc. Just like any other lad, I was given jobs like taking the wheelbarrow out to deliver magazines, but eventually I learnt the art of "composing" - setting up the type into a "stick". I helped type-set the magazines, and learnt something about the trade, but it was very poorly paid. At the age of 21 I was only earning about 10/- a week.

That wasn't good enough for me, so I left, and went to Whiteheads, a very good commercial printer in Wolverhampton. I stayed there for about three years, in which time I got married, but we struck a period of recession, and I found myself being put on short time. It was 1936 or 1937, and I thought I would try and get a job with the Express and Star. I went to see the Overseer of the Composing Room, at his home address, and he said I could start as soon as I had served my fortnight's notice at Whiteheads.

John Hartland, was a marvellous man: a man who could take complete control of a composing room. He was responsible for seeing that the work was done so that each edition of the paper came out on time. Such was his authority that if a story arrived from the editorial department at the very last minute, he had the confidence to tear it up and throw it in the bin, simply saying,"It's too bloody late!"

He arrived at ten and left at five, leaving his deputy to take command for the first and last hour of each working day. On Monday mornings his arrival was followed by an inspection of the L-shaped composing room. One Monday he said to me, "My laddie, are you married?"
I said, "Yes Sir."
"Well," he replied, "get your wife to wash your apron. Make sure it's a clean apron every Monday morning!"
Although he was such a firm figure, the atmosphere in the composing room was such that we would all help each other, and it was a good place in which to work.

The type was set in Lino-type machines, not letter by letter in loose pieces of type, but in lines of type cast in hot metal. The metal itself was very hot, but the ends of our fingers hardened and were accostomed to handling it. It was a clean process, much better than handling individual pieces of dirty type. Most noticable was the speed at which we had to work, and our greatest priority was keeping to the deadlines relating to each edition of the paper. I think the Stafford edition came out at 1.30., followed by the District at 2.15., followed by others at frequent intervals through to 5.30. or 6.00.pm.

The story came through from the editorial department onto the Overseer's desk. If it was a big story, like the front page leading story, he would break it up into small sections, naming them A1,A2,A3 and so on. He would give the headlines to us compositors, and the sections of text would be distributed among the Lino-type operators. As soon as the sections were completed they were dropped onto the "random". The man in charge of the random would then assemble the sections of the story in the correct order, pull a proof and send it to the proof readers. A proof was also sent to the editorial department, and to the editor. The completed story would then be taken down to the "stone". If the headline was ready, the whole thing could be put into its proper position in the page. Providing there was time it could be corrected - if required.

We had an efficient reading staff, who were very clever at doing their job, but I have always been mystified by how they read their copy. If a mistake was made, the whole line had to be set again. Two men usually worked on a page while it was on the stone - one changing the stories for each edition, and one working on the corrections.

When a page was complete, and made solid by being locked into its "chase" - the metal frame in which it was contained, it was pushed through a partition to the foundry. The foundry had a hot press that compressed the type into a "flong", the sheet of papier mache that bore a female impression of the page which could then be put into a round cylinder to cast the plates that went straight onto the printing machines.

As soon as the flong was made, the page returned to the stone, although still very hot. The stone hands would then have to work on the page as it was modified for each edition. It was very hot work. If a story that had to be removed from the page was likely to be used again in a later edition, it had to be kept by you, but if the story was not going to be used again it could be thrown in the "pie bin". In a commercial office, using loose type, the pie bin would then have to be emptied and each piece of type would have to be sorted into the appropriate section of the right tray - a different tray for each font. But in a newspaper office the pieces of Lino-type from the pie bin are taken back to the foundry and melted down to make lead which will provide hot metal for the Lino-type machines the next day.

On the stone, you would usually find that the adverts were in place first thing in the morning, because they had usually been set the previous afternoon or evening. The Advertising Department worked out where they should go on the page, but they sometimes made mistakes like putting competitors alongside each other, and we could use our initiative in changing such things. We also had to assemble the "smalls" - the small advertisements, and these had to put in the correct order on the page. The order was: Hatches, Matches and Despatches - in other words, Births, Marriages and Deaths. And there were many other refinements to putting smalls in order. For example, you could not say that the deceased was remembered by his son before saying that he was remembered by his widow. Even if some of them were set the previous day, they were all mixed up in the galleys, and we had to be pretty slick to sort out the columns and columns of the paper occupied by smalls.

One morning I was sorting out the smalls, and I came across an ad selling a kit of tumblers. I put it in the correct place - among the "Horses, Dogs and Poultry". The Overseer came down when he saw the proof to tell me that it should be put in "Sales by Miscellaneous Contract", and that I ought to know better. It took me some time to convince him that "tumblers" were pigeons!

If the afternoons were totally occupied producing the various editions, we would have to work overtime

The composing room at the Express & Star, Wolverhampton, in the 1930's. In the right foreground Arthur Baldwin is pulling a proof on the small proof press, and will despatch the proofs via the hatches on his right. Behind him Jack Elkin and an apprentice are working on the random, putting the typesetting into correct order, arranging the columns and putting in the headlines. On the extreme left is a row of Lino-type machine operators, and in the background one of the operators is coming down the aisle to the random with a handful of "slugs" - the lines of lead type produced by the machines.

to set the next day's adverts, and often the copy would not arrive until the last minute. But overtime was pleasant - that was when we had most fun. That was time when we compositors were left to ourselves, a time when we could enjoy a joke. The Overseer was a very good snuff-taker, printers are generally good snuff-takers and beer drinkers, although I am a teetotaller. The Overseer had a very special kind of snuff, and in the afternoon he would send for more supplies to fill his box. I'm sure he turned a blind eye to the fact that his box was regularly raided during overtime.

Some stone hands could not even set their own name in type, and a Lino-type operator knew little about making up a page, but we compositors knew both jobs, and stood in for them if they were away. Sometimes we could develop a good understanding with the editorial staff as well. For example, I could often anticipate what the Sports Editor, George Gillott, was going to write, and if he miscalculated and a headline would not go in, I could alter it myself, and he would invariably approve the alteration.

A new Works Manager came, and eventually he sent for me and offered me the new position of Chief Compositor. A day later I accepted and I was put in charge of the ten compositors. We had to work hard, and we had to work as a team. I'm sure I cussed them at times, but they took it, and they must have made our spirit of co-operation possible. I think we did a good job.

I enjoyed my work, and never minded going to it. At election time we worked from Thursday morning to Friday night without stopping - but we never minded at all. It was a six-day week that finished with the production of the Sports paper on Saturday night, and we did not work on Good Friday or Christmas Day. On one Good Friday we were playing for our football team and Ethiopia was invaded so we were called in to produce a special edition! In the early days of my career, we had one day off a fortnight during the winter. Later this was extended to all year round, and eventually we worked a five day week.

Life at the paper was very sociable, and I became the first Chairman of the new Social Club. I remember a trip we organised for over six hundred staff to London at the time of the Festival of Britain - even Mr.Graham, the paper's proprietor came along. And that's how I enjoyed working there for almost forty years.

I retired just before the technology of newspaper production really began to change. The Express and Star has always prided itself of being in the forefront of technical development, but I don't think I could have adapted to the new technology. In the old days of hot metal we worked with our fingers and our brains, but now the story arrives on a piece of paper, it is cut out with a scalpel and placed in position - to me that's not like doing work at all.

7

SERVING THE CUSTOMER

"There's one of mine"

Dennis Whitehouse

In my Grandfather's time the family were master builders with a business in Princes End and my father, Harry Whitehouse, began serving an apprenticeship as a bricklayer for his father. However, he was laid off for for a period of about fourteen weeks during a long severe frost and he was told to find another job. He found one at the local hairdresser, and that's how he got into hairdressing.

Having served his time in Princes End he became a journeyman in Smethwick, and then started his own business in Pleck, before the First World War. Harry Whitehouse joined up in 1915, and this led to the closure of the business in Pleck. He was taken prisoner of war in 1917. In fact, my mother was informed that he was "missing - presumed killed". She received the normal telegram telling her. She waited for three months for confirmation of that, but did not receive it. She was short of cash and struggling to bring up my brother, so when someone came along who wanted to buy the shop, she sold it. Two months later she learned that he was a prisoner of war. Of course, when he came back he found the business had gone!

He had to get a job so he went back to Smethwick, where he had been a journeyman, and it was from there, in 1920, that he moved. He bought the hairdressing shop at 415 Dudley Road, Wolverhampton, that had belonged to a man called Harry Edge. The family moved to Myrtle Street, by Parkfield Road, and my father walked from there to the shop every day.

I first worked in my father's shop while I was still at school, and was a lather boy and general handyman. I left school at fourteen, in 1937, but there was insufficient trade for me to join my father full time. At that time there were about ten barbers' shops along the Dudley Road, from Snow Hill to the Fighting Cocks. There was one within two hundred yards of our premises. Therefore, I went to work for the Co-op as a grocery assistant, and stayed there until I was called up in 1942, during the Second World War. In the meantime I had spent my weekends doing hairdressing and helping out whenever I could, so I acquired a working knowledge of the trade.

Having joined the Navy in 1942, I was away for four years, but during that time I realised there was

Above: Steven Banks demonstrates the Dart overhead cash carrier still in use at Harry Cooper's menswear shop in Willenhall in 1986, a year before the business closed.

an opportunity for me to make a bob or two. My father sent me some tools, and all the time I was in the Navy, on all the ships I was on, I was cutting hair. Even when I went to a shore station in Russia I was still cutting hair and supplementing my Services pay. I had taken some scissors, comb and hand clippers with me, but my father was able to send me some German-made electric clippers. They reached me in Russia via the mail!

Electric clippers were in their infancy, and the first time I switched them on they ruined the reception on all the radio sets in that Arctic transmitting station. I wasn't very popular and was severely sat on by the Chief Petty Officer Telegraphist, and told to switch my bloody clippers off! However, we had a radio mechanic who was able to build a supressor unit, and this enabled me to give a haircut with my clippers to anyone who wanted one even when working in the transmitting station.

I returned to Wolverhampton in 1946. In a way the War had been good for my Father's business because the younger men in the trade had been called away leaving the older men, such as himself, a larger slice of the trade. Thus, in 1946, he was sufficiently busy for me to be able to join him in the business, and we worked together for three years, until he died in 1949.

Along with my father, and a few other people in the town, I helped to start the first local branch of the National Hairdressers' Federation. We set up a scheme to train our apprentices in the shops, and established a small "academy" in one of the big saloons in town. Apprentices could go to this in an evening, after work, and be trained in doing the modern styles. This was the forerunner to all the training that goes on today. About twenty apprentices took part and all helped in training each other.

It's a funny trade to learn: if you are a carpenter you can practice on a piece of wood, or a tailor can practice on a piece of cloth, but a hairdresser has to get it right first time. The first few months of an apprentice's life is virtually spent just handling the tools. It's very boring and the lads think you're being funny telling them to put a comb or scissors in their hand just to get the feel of them. You have to acquire confidence in using an open razor and learn how much feel to put into it. We used to lather up a balloon marked out with a face, tied to the headrest of a chair. You had to remove the lather from the balloon, and if the balloon burst you knew that you were too heavy handed!

It can take several months sitting at a stone learning to sharpen a razor, and its worth taking the time to get it right because, funnily enough, a blunt razor is more likely to cut a customer than a sharp one. Normally an apprentice first shaves a relative or the proprietor of the saloon. The first person I ever shaved was my father. His beard was quite tough. and as I shaved him, trembling in my shoes, he used to kick me on my ankle to indicate whether I was using the razor correctly or not.

It's very tricky letting the apprentice loose on the customers. I used to select pensioners whom I knew weren't very well off, and say, "Look, you can have this haircut on the house - if you'll let the apprentice have a go!" Even then I would have to check the apprentice didn't make a God Almighty mess of it. If the carpenter's apprentice makes a mess with a bit of wood you can throw it away and start again, but you can't do that with a customer's head, can you? And an apprentice has to learn more than just how to cut hair - he has to learn how to deal with people.

Sitting in a chair having your hair cut is very relaxing, and that is why folk come in and talk about such a wide variety of things, and the customers themselves can be all sorts of people. Once when the local factory was on strike we used to be listening to the management one minute, and a chap from the striking workforce the next. A barber certainly knows a lot of what's going on in his area, and he has to treat what he hears with confidentiality - you have to keep your mouth shut.

Once I had a manager come in from one of the local factories to find one of his men having a quick haircut in works time. I found out afterwards that that the manager had given the man a ticking-off, to which the man had replied, "But it grows in works time!" "Ah - but not all of it", pointed out the manager. But the worker was not to be beaten by this and said, ""Well, I haven't had it all cut!"

I once had a policeman sitting in the chair when there was a knock at the back door. When I opened it, I found a chap selling rugs and blankets. I declined to buy any but when I returned to the copper and told him about it, he said, "Get this gown off me, I've been after him for bloody years!" - and he dived round the corner and pinched him.

The satisfaction was in doing the job - feeling it was a proper craft. Up until the years after the War there had only been a few shops that could give a really

Above: Dennis Whitehouse, on the left, outside his Gents Hair Dressing shop at 415 Dudley Road, Wolverhampton, in the 1950's. (Pete Whitehouse collection)

good haircut. Many shops were real back street affairs. But, through the Federation, training was taken seriously. the idea behind setting up the NHF was to try and regulate the standard of hairdressing being done. Even so, the trade has always been a bit of a free for all. We sat on a committee with the Local Authority to set a standard Code of Practice and Code of Hygiene that could be put into the local bye-laws.

The heyday of the business was in the mid fifties, and even into the sixties in the area we were in. It was an old Victorian shop and it became due for demolition. New flats and a shopping precinct were built in Blakenhall, and soon afterwards my shop was demolished. I was offered a new shop in the precinct by the Corporation, which I took up, and the business moved two hundred yards. It was a good precinct in which to work up until about five years ago, but then I felt the area began to deteriorate.

If my Dad came back today to see how the trade was getting on, I think he would be surprised to find "Unisex" saloons, but perhaps he would be even more surprised to meet customers who want their hair dyed red, white and blue, or want their hair to stand up on end, or even want it all shaved off. I think it would offend his sense of tradesmanship. He always used to tell me he could recognise his own haircuts - but I've found it to be true. If you do a good job, you can be walking down the street, see a chap's head, and think, "There's one of mine." You are proud to have done the work.

Dennis Whitehouse died in December 1989, and he knew that he was very ill when he agreed to provide this account of his career. His son, Pete Whitehouse, has allowed it to be used in this book.

Above: Kent Street, Upper Gornal, Branch of the Dudley Co-operative Society, about 1936. Left to right: Sid Rollason, Jack Evans, Bill Watton, Jim Percy, Mr.Bright, the manager, with his wife seated in front of him, Mr.Jeavons, Lily Baker, unknown, Jim Hodgetts and Richard Smout. (Connie Beach collection)

Working at the Co-Op

Lily Tighe, nee Baker.

When I left school, at the age of fourteen, my Father wanted me to stay at home to help Mother, but then, in 1915, he had to go into the Army. I was dead keen to start work, and the week after my Father joined the Army, in the July, I applied for a job at the Co-op. I had always wanted to work in a grocery shop, but there was a time I wished I never had!

At the time the General Manager of the Dudley Co-operative Society was Mr.Harry Crew and the Secretary was Mr.Benjamin Pearson. (They lived in the houses in Waddam's Pool, Hall Street, where the Society had its Head Offices.) I had to go to the shop in Kent Street, Upper Gornal, and was interviewed by the General Manager, in the garden outside the store, while I sat on a Tate and Lyle sugar box. I was given the job and started work on a Thursday.

The following Monday was supposed to be a Bank Holiday but the holiday was cancelled. Unfortunately, I was feeling "wonky" and wasn't able to go in. When I returned on the Tuesday, the manager growled, "Are you often like this?" but I don't think I had any further sick leave during the twenty two years that I worked there.

The manager of the branch was Mr.Hadlington. His temper was rather uneven, but he gave me a marvellous training. This involved learning to weigh and wrap virtually everything. Very little was pre-packed. We weighed and packed the sugar, rice, dried fruit, etc, and at the back of the shop we weighed out corn, bran, oats, malt, and sharps - a brown powder that could be made into a paste when preparing food for fowl. The weighing of malt covered us with dust, and we

also had to contend with rats. We even weighed tobacco twist: thick, medium and thin.

Mr.Hadlington was an expert at wrapping goods - he could do it better than a machine could have done, but he had very set ideas about how things should be done. One young man set out to make patterns with pieces of cheese cut up and put on display, but Mr.Hadlington didn't approve of that!

He reckoned that he would never grow rich while working for the Co-op, so he and his wife eventually left and opened a business in Bridgnorth Road, Wollaston.

For years I was the only female member of staff and I worked on the grocery counter. I was only very rarely allowed to work on the provisions counter, where the manager presided over the bacon slicer. I had been very poor at arithmetic at school, but learnt to reckon up groceries very well. We had our own tills and were responsible for balancing our copies of the checks against the money we had taken. Mr.Hadlington was very strict about reckoning-up and if you made an error amounting to a halfpenny it was more than your life was worth. One Wednesday (Early closing day) I was a pound out - and it had to be taken out of my wages. We worked from about eight in the morning until six at night, and I have always remembered my first week's wages: it was six shillings.

We had boys to make deliveries of milk and bread. It surprised me how much the bread was handled. It was baked in North Street at Waddam's Pool, and was brought to the back of our shop where the large

Making Deliveries
Right: Howard Cook and the bicycle used for deliveries from Cliff Evans' butchers shop, Enville Road, Wall Heath, 1961. (John Guttery)

Making Deliveries
Right: Thomas Turvey and his horse drawn milk float. From a yard at 9 Price Street, West Bromwich, he delivered milk to the Herbert Street-Beecher Road-Birmingham Road area of West Bromwich. The milk was brought from Wellington by his brother-in-law, John Morris, in large churns, and was transferred to smaller churns to take out on the float. Thomas received a gold watch in 1916 from the West Bromwich Dairymen's Association "for services rendered", and is seen here winning second prize in a local dairy show. On 30 July 1913 he and "Kitty" won first prize in the Tradesmen's Light Horse Section of the West Bromich Horse Show in Dartmouth Park. (Stan Wilkins)

Making Deliveries
Right: Delivering milk in bottles began in the 1930's. Terry McGovern is seen here delivering milk in Gornal Wood for the Central Midlands Co-operative Society in July 1989.

rats lurked. The boys then put the loaves into basket carriages to make the local deliveries.

Eventually my duties took me out of the shop two days a week - all Monday and Tuesday I spent getting orders from quite a big round. I used to walk to work from my home in St.James Terrace, Eve Hill, and then set out, not returning to the shop until the end of the afternoon. I went to Woodsetton. Eve Lane, the Upper Gornal Housing Scheme, Parkes Hall, Hurst Hill, and even down to Roseville. I collected the money for the previous week's delivery and collected the current week's order, took checks back in and worked out customers' dividends. The deliveries themselves were usually made by van, on a Thursday afternoon. At one stage I also took orders for coal.

Some customers were tempted to get into debt as far as coal was concerned, and one of my duties was to try to collect this debt. On one occasion a lady wrapped pennies in silver paper to try and convince me they were half crowns. Sometimes people tried to swing the lead, but we did not let people get into debt.

In the twenty two years that I spent at the branch I worked with three managers, and saw the shop rebuilt on the same site. After Mr.Hadlington left, he was replaced with Mr.Bright. Mr. and Mrs. Bright were a lovely couple - "bright" by name and by nature. He was not a very tall man but he used to tell us, "The small ones get to where the big ones can't get in". Lastly I worked with Mr.Mills who lived on the Upper Gornal Housing Scheme, unlike his predecessors who had lived on the premises. In all that time I only worked elsewhere on one occasion - I was once sent to Sedgley for a few days. Perhaps I was kept at the branch to show the new managers the ropes!

I left when I was thirty seven, and started my family. Mr.Benjamin Pearson gave me a two-tier cake stand, and the staff at the branch gave me a coffee set. It has always amazed me how I learned to reckon-up after having been so poor at arithmetic at school, and, when I look back, I think what I enjoyed most was being out on those rounds.

Life on the Mobile

John Guttery

When I was still at school I had a part-time job with the local Co-op shop. I used to deliver the meat on a bike, and on Friday nights and Saturday mornings I would end up scrubbing the block in the shop. At the age of fifteen, in 1958, I started full-time at the Wall Heath Branch of the Co-op, which is now closed. I stayed there two years and then went to work for another butcher in the High Street: Wilson's. About a year later I moved to Cliff Evans' in Enville Road.

When I was about nineteen and a half the Departmental Manager of the Co-op came to see me and asked if I would like to work on a "mobile" - a van adapted as a travelling butcher's shop, delivering meat to the customers in their own streets. I said, "Yes, I'll give it a go."

The Dudley Co-operative Society had four mobiles, one of which was a spare. One worked from the Butchery Dept. at Nith Place, one worked from the branch at Kates Hill, and I was to take over the van that worked from the branch in Ridge Road, Kingswinford. (Even that branch has totally disappeared now and there are houses on the site.)

I had to catch the six o'clock bus to be able to collect the van from Ridge Road each morning. The sides of meat had to be collected from Nith Place once a week, and brought down to the branch, and on a daily basis I had to collect the loins of pork, cut pork, pies and sausages etc. At one time the Co-op made their own pies, sausages, boiled tongue etc. at Nith Place, but later they bought these things from a wholesaler. Back at Ridge Road, I had to load the motor for the day's round, and then off I would go.

For the first two weeks a chap came with me who showed me the round, and then I worked by myself. The first week we went out we took £500, which seemed a lot of money to me at the time, but when I took the round over by myself I found I was able to increase the business. People that knew me when I had worked at Wilson's and Evans' became my new customers on the mobile. There was quite a lot involved in the job: driving the van, preparing the meat, going out in search of customers, taking the money and keeping the books, but I found that I enjoyed it. Although I had managers above me, I had a free hand once I was out on the round and no-one was looking over my shoulder.

Even now it is still hard work, and we start work early, but once the work is done: that's that. It's not like working in a shop. Monday was usually a half day, but now I don't go out on Mondays at all. Tuesday was and is a heavier day. Wednesdays and Thursdays are often over by lunchtime. The two busiest days are Friday and Saturday. Most customers paid for the meat as they bought it, but some liked it "put on the book". Like some other butchers, I still run a "book" today. Customers settle up for all the meat they have had during the week on Saturdays, and then say, "Put today's meat on the book, John." It is paid for the following weekend, and that's how it goes on...

Left: John Guttery on "the mobile", 1990.

In the early eighties I had the feeling that the Co-op was going to close down, so I decided that I would like to work for myself. Of course I needed a base to work from, and suddenly an opportunity arose. Steve Edwards, who had taken over Wilson's business, offered me the use of his fridge, mincer, meat slicers etc for so much a week. I had been to the Meat-Ex shows at the NEC and seen mobiles, so I looked in the Meat Trades Journal to see how much I would have to pay for a second-hand vehicle. The mobiles are made by two or three firms in Scotland, where mobile shops are still much more common. One Thursday I took a day off from the Co-op and flew up to Glasgow. At the factory I was shown the Ford Transit that was waiting for me - all done up, and all the sign-writing completed for me. I drove it back home, finished the week for the Co-op, and then left.

It was the July of 1981 that I started work in my first mobile, and about six months later the Co-op closed. The funny thing was that for that six months both me and the Co-op were competing with each other for trade in the same area. I am still working the same round today, but three or four years ago we replaced the Ford Transit with a Bedford. Two other chaps from the Co-op also run mobiles - based on a shop in Tividale, but apart from that there aren't many mobiles around today.

My wife, Joan, has always helped me with the business, and for twelve months my son helped me. Apart from things like occasionally getting stuck in the snow, we thoroughly enjoy it. My customers have been very loyal to me. In fact, they are more like friends - and now I am selling to the grown-up children of my first customers. People set their watches by my arrival. On Saturday mornings my first customers in Kingswinford expect to see me by a quarter to eight. If I arrive at ten to eight, its "John, you're late aren't you?"

The one thing we dread is that, in cold weather, the van won't start. If that happens we put on a tow rope attached to the back of our car. We pull her along for a few yards, and off she goes. Once the van was off the road for a week, and it was an absolute nightmare trying to collect orders and make deliveries using the car.

People don't seem to eat as much meat as they used to. I don't think people make a stew when they can buy convenience food from supermarkets, so we have diversified a little. We sell tinned goods, cheese etc., and we make our own beefburgers and barbecue packs. We don't have time to make faggots or boil tongues. Our meat is very reasonable compared with what people pay in supermarkets, and we take a pride in the quality of the meat and the presentation of the mobile etc.

When people come out of their home to buy something from a mobile they often seem to lock themselves out of the house. I have often had to climb in through a window to let a customer back into the home. Once a woman locked herself out and all the downstairs windows were closed. There was a bedroom fanlight window open so we had to search the neighbourhood for a ladder, and then find some way of lifting the catch. After all that I realised that she had a Staffordshire Bull Terrier in the house, so I insisted that she went up the ladder and climbed in through the window!

I even had one customer who was confined to the top floor of her house. She lowered a bucket from a window to collect her meat, and used the same bucket to drop the money down to me. After dealing with all these things I am still expected to keep up with my schedule, perform a few extra tasks like posting letters for the old folk, and never miss a day's work. I have occasionally allowed myself to go on holiday, but I have to give the customers plenty of warning so that they can stock up. The nice thing about it is that if we return from holiday broke, we usually follow it with a very good week on the round.

Right: Mobile shops are now fairly rare in the Black Country, but John Guttery has been on the road in his mobile butchers shop since July 1981. His spotless cream and blue van travels the western border lands of the Black Country with a personal service in the tradition of the retailer coming to the customer.

Fresh Veg

Edna Micklewright

I've been on this stall at Willenhall Market, working for Bob King, since 1976, but really I've been in the trade all my life. Fifty nine years ago I started working in a greengrocer's shop in Green Lane, Walsall, and I've always worked on the veg side rather than with the fruit. When I started I was working for Len King, who was the brother of Bob's Grand-dad - so I have always worked for the same family.

When I started we began work at half past six in the morning, and could still be serving at half past ten at night, and we worked seven days a week, because we opened on Sunday mornings. I "lived in", so I was there at everybody's beck and call, but I worked there about twentyfive years. I left when I had my family, and returned to the trade when they grew up.

Twenty two years ago Bob's uncle rang me, and offered me a job in his shop at the Delves, but I didn't like it there - it was too slow for me. A place became available on the stall in Walsall Market, but I was reluctant to take it as I had never worked on a stall before. They persuaded me to go and I found I liked it. Bob was running the stall two days a week at the time, on Tuedays and Fridays, but he had to move when his cousin came of age in 1976. Bob was offered this stall in Willenhall, so he took it over, and I came with him.

I found that I preferred Willenhall Market to the one at Walsall. At Walsall just about every other stall was selling fruit and veg - and they were all related to one another! Here at Willenhall we are on our own. That means there is more chance of being busy, and that suits me because I like to be on the go all the while. At first I worked the three days - Wednesday, Friday and Saturday, but when I found that was too much for me I started doing two days. Wednesday is not busy enough for me so I like to work Fridays and Saturdays.

I've been going to retire ever since I was sixty, but Bob tells me I'm not old enough yet. I'm 72 now but I still love the work, and feel I would really miss it if I had to give it up. Its the sort of work that gets me out of myself, because it's dealing with people all day long. I don't do the pitching out or packing up - I just come along for the bit in the middle. I start about a quarter past eight and go just after four, but they start setting up the stall at half past four in the morning.

Some parts of the year are busier than others. It's busy when the strawberries and peaches arrive, but it is quiet late summer. It gets busier on the run up to Christmas, and at that time of year we sell things like holly wreaths. I'm used to being out all weathers, and have been through some really bad winters.

I have got to know my customers - the regulars are smashing. I can hear them telling each other that I'm the best one to look after them, and they come back to me week after week. If I think something will not suit them, I advise them not to buy, and I tend to know what they are going to want. For example, I know that about six to eight regulars are going to come for cauliflowers, so I put some really good ones to one side - under the stall - and save them for them. Mind you, Bob has really good stuff, and it is his policy that the stock is as good at the back of the stall as it is at the front. That's why people come back to us.

The goods is very beautifully displayed, and when you've been setting it out since four thirty in the morning you don't want people mauling it about. We don't let people pick the stuff up. If they do, we tell them to go to a self-service store. About ten years ago I remember a lady grabbing a spring cabbage. When you pick one of them up, all leaves fall off if not properly handled. She was not pleased when Bob told her to put it down and quite a row developed. She went away and returned with a big knife, ready to murder us. We laugh about it now, but it was not funny at the time. If I am ever weighing a spring cabbage for

Left: Edna Micklewright serving vegetables from King's market stall, Willenhall, in 1986

Right: Trading in Willenhall market 1986

Bob, he will still say, "Don't mention 'spring cabbage' to me!"

Our stall looks very artistic first thing in the morning, but there is not much packing away to do at the end of the day because we try to stock just the right amount of stuff to sell out by the end of the afternoon. And, if it's going well, I am busy all day. In fact, I quite like a queue, as long as I'm not having to dash about selling fruit as well as the veg.

I don,t think the work has changed much. One of the biggest things we had to face was decimilisation. I was on Walsall Market at the time, and I can re-member pleading to be sacked, saying, "I can't do this - I'll have to leave - I'll never understand it!" Now we would never be able to change back. For some time after that happened, the old ladies used to give me their purses, to take out the correct money and put the change in.

I hope I can go on working, but when it comes to markets I'm just a youngster. There are many people who have worked on stalls all their lives. There is one chap here at Willenhall who is sixty, and his father had the stall for years before, so there must be many people on markets with a tale to tell.

Right: George Codd, once a well known figure in Wolverhampton's Retail Market, photographed trying to convince a Wulfrunian that she should buy (and consume) whale meat, during the Second World War. (Eileen Codd's collection)

8

MADE IN THE BLACK COUNTRY

The Last Heat

Bill Harris

Steel-making in the Black Country didn't cease with the closure of the big works like Bilston, Round Oak, and Patent Shaft, but it has ceased now that the "Mini Mill" at the Triplex-Lloyd works at James Bridge has closed. After thirty four years of making steel, I'm having to learn a new trade: welding it.

I worked at the Patent Shaft Steel Works for twenty four years, starting on the gas furnaces. They were converted to oil furnaces and then the electric furnaces were built, and I worked on them until the end. Originally the Shaft employed a First, Second, Third and Fourth Hand on a furnace, but later they did away with the Fourth Hand and had a "utility man", who could help out on either of the furnaces. I worked my way up from mineral loading to First Hand, step by step. When I first went to the Shaft it took years to climb that ladder - you had to wait for someone to die before you could advance - but, as time went by, promotion came more quickly.

The First Hand was responsible for the furnace and making the steel. He would take samples when it was ready and send them down to the lab. The results would come back and he would add lime or introduce oxygen to blow the carbon out, and maintain the correct temperature.

I was on nights when we finished at the Shaft, and left on the Thursday night. I went for an interview at F.H.Lloyds on the Friday morning, and started there on the following Monday. I was very sorry to leave Patent Shaft, and had never believed that it would ever close. It was so much a part of Wednesbury, and we felt that as long as there was work at the Shaft, there would be work everywhere. After I started at Lloyds, I was sent back to the Shaft to collect something for them. I walked around the place where I had worked, and everything was just as we had left it - the cups were still on the tables where we had had a drink. That was heart-breaking.

I was offered a job at Wiggin Alloys, and one at Bars & Braces, Great Bridge, on small furnaces, but I went to Lloyds because they were starting a new mill. In fact, I was the first employed in their new mill. The new furnace was made in Italy, and I un-

In "Black Country Folk at Werk" a section was devoted to the iron and steel industry, and another section was devoted to local manufacturing, both in metal, and a variety of materials - wood, leather, glass etc. These strands are brought together in this section, where, once again, working with metal dominates everything else. Producing iron and steel, as opposed to making it into something else, still merits a whole book to itself, but meanwhile we begin this section with an account by the man who produced the last Black Country steel, at F.H.Lloyd's steel making plant at James Bridge, Darlaston, on 27 April 1990. Above: First hand melter, Bill Harris, shakes the hand of Works Director, Alan Johnson, as the plant closes with the loss of 180 jobs. Once F.H.Lloyds were a major producer of engineering steels and castings, employing over 5000 people. The company started life in 1879, in Wednesbury, and on the James Bridge site it became the first commercial producer of steel castings in the country. Less than twenty years ago the site was still producing 25,000 tonnes of steel annually. Now the site will redeveloped as part of the new cleaner Black Country.

loaded it from the wagons as it arrived, and then helped to build it. When it was ready for production, I was put on as First Hand.

On a modern electric furnace we were able to tap about forty two tons every two hours, but, of course no two heats are the same, so sometimes it took longer. We worked in the normal way, taking a sample, infiltrating oxygen, or adding lime, but we would then add manganese to meet the specification of the required steel. The steel was scanned before it could go into the casting machine - eventually coming out as a billet.

As soon as it was tapped, another heat would be started. The furnace would be repaired, re-charged, and we started again. It was very different to the old

74

days when a heat sometimes lasted for twelve to four- teen hours before it could be tapped. Sometimes a shift was over before your heat was tapped.

When I started the mill, I thought I would be spend- ing the rest of my working life there, but it only lasted ten years - I was disappointed. People had come to LLoyds from Round Oak, Patent Shaft, and a few from Bilston - people who had been in the steel trade for a long while. Our steel went out to local firms like Seamless Tubes, but now they have to get their steel from Sheffield. The new mill occupied the old Heavy Foundry shop on the F.H.Lloyd site, and a new rolling mill was put into the machine shop, where steel had once been sent from all over Britain to be machined. But I think we were doomed, because obviously they wanted to redevelop the whole site that had once been occupied by the foundry and engineering business - and the steel could be made elsewhere.

Pat Roach came down one day to start the demoli- tion of one of the old F.H.Lloyd buildings, by swinging the hammer into it. He said to us, "Now it looks like the Black Hole of Calcutta as you come off the motor- way, but we're going to make it the Golden Gateway of the Midlands."

I took samples from the last heat, and gave those samples to people as souvenirs - little "lollipop" shaped samples, which people have polished and mounted on a piece of wood, enscribed with the words, "Made in the Last Heat", and dated 25/4/90. I've kept a couple myself, and somewhere I have similar samples of the last steel made at Patent Shaft.

Steelworkers are often very "close", and many are related to each other. Many fathers, brothers, wives etc. have worked in the same place. I first lived in Tipton, but I married a girl who worked at the Shaft and moved to Wednesbury. Her father worked there, and in the last couple of years, my son-in-law has worked at LLoyd's. Even he feels that it is heartbreak- ing to stop making steel. But we all keep in contact with each other, and we shall keep the Fishing Club going to keep us together.

Going Through The Mill

Archie Clarke

Baldwin's Steel Works at Swindon was well known locally. The mills, where red hot bars were rolled into thin sheets, could be heard rumbling like distant thunder two miles away. At night, when the sky was lit by flashes of light from the open furnaces, it was like an artillery barrage.

In 1934, at the age of sixteen, after working in various other departments, I moved into the mills. Before starting the new job, I bought a new pair of clogs and several cotton vests with low necks and short sleeves. With thin trousers, and a towel as a sweatcloth, this was the normal working dress for all mill workers. The wooden clogs, with irons like miniature horse shoes on sole and heel, were essential for working on steel floors that became very hot.

The mills worked continuously from Monday morning to Saturday lunchtime in three shifts: 5.30.am. to 1.30.pm., 1.30.pm. to 9.30.pm. and 9.30.pm. to 5.30.am. The reason for these odd finishing times was to allow workers to obtain a drink at the end of the morning and afternoon shifts, as pubs closed at 2.00.pm. and 10.00.pm. We changed shift every week, and it took me some time to adapt to working in this way.

The morning shift was best, but rising at 4.30.am. on a cold winter morning, washing in cold water, then waiting for the kettle to boil on the newly lit fire, was not the best way to start a day. When the shift ended, I rode home on my bike, washed, ate, then usually slept for an hour or more, and was ready to go out with friends for the evening. It was the only shift that enabled me to enjoy the whole evening.

There were six mills, varying in size from Number 1, which rolled the smaller sheets, to Number 6, which produced sheets 8ft.x 4ft. Each mill consisted of a pair of rolls, each weighing several tons, and mounted one above the other. Over the necks of the rolls were two large screws, operated by heavy steel handles, which turned the slotted heads of the screws. As bars were fed through the rolls, the screws were revolved to keep the pressure on them. Every mill was serviced by two furnaces: one heated bars, the other re-heated packs after the first rolling.

A magnificent steam engine drove the six pairs of rolls. This powerful monster worked for twentyfour hours each day, for five and a half days of every week. During that time it stopped for about fifteen minutes, three times a day, when the shifts changed. During the three years I worked in the mills, it was shut down for a small repair only twice, and each stop lasted less than an hour.

Like all youths who started in the mills, my first job was "holding down". When a pair of bars had been rolled into plates about two metres in length, they were pulled into the doubling area behind the rolls. The "doubler", who was few years older than me, then took over. With his tongs he separated the two plates. This took quite an effort, and the plates were hot enough to burn if touched. We lifted the top plate aside and put the bottom plate on top of it. I then held one corner, and he took the one at the opposite end. He then stepped over the plates towards me, bringing his end of the plates to meet mine. He pressed his corner down, and as the two corners met, I grabbed

Below and opposite: The installation of Galloway's steam driven hot rolling mill plant at Baldwin's Steel Works, Swindon, about 1913. In the picture on the opposite page, the "works manager", Tom Jones, occupied the left foreground. (May Griffiths collection)

both with my tongs. The plates were now bent double and held by one corner, but were rounded like an oval balloon. To flatten them sufficiently to pass under the press, the doubler stepped on to the rounded plates and jumped on them. This created the "pack" - which I pushed under the press, which flattened it completely, then dragged it to the shear blade and cropped the open edge straight. The pack was then collected by the "bar dragger", and was taken back to the furnace for re-heating.

The combined punch and shearing machine was called "the Crocodile". It was at floor level, and worked continuously, as the press descended the shear blade at the other end rose, and opened like a crocodile's mouth. When the press rose, the "mouth" closed. The following year, when I had become the doubler, I realised how dangerous the crocodile could be.

I had only two mishaps during the year that I spent doubling, which was a good average considering that I was jumping on steel two feet above the ground, about eighty times a shift. As I fell the first time, my arm went under the press just as it was rising. I relived that split second many times, and, as the "holder-down" said, "Ah bet yo've never moved so fast in yer life." The second fall resulted in a badly burned arm from contact with the floor, resulting in two weeks "on the box". (i.e. - unable to work as a result of the injury)

The one hundred and fifty men who worked in the mills did not have to clock in, because they were not paid by the hour for their attendance. They were simply paid for every ton of steel that they processed. There was great competition between different mills, and different shifts. The first question that everybody asked as they arrived was what weight had been produced on the previous shift, and the weights produced by their rivals? How the prices for the different steels were fixed I do not know, but during the time I spent in the mills they did not alter.

In 1936, after much discussion, the local trade union secretary held a meeting in "The Bush", one of the three pubs in Swindon. At the end of the morning shift most of the men crowded into a room and heard an explanation of the benefits of membership. I was most impressed by the way in which the union fought for compensation for industrial injuries. I decided the subscription was a cheap insurance premium, and joined the union along with the majority of the men. Up until that time very few of the men had been members of the union, but when I left the company a year later most of the mill workers had joined.

Each mill was manned by six men and two youths, the doubler and the holder-down. In charge of the two youths was the Shearer, who sheared the packs of sheets to a rough size while they were still hot. The doubler was his assistant. Using the steam-driven shears was not precision work but nevertheless it was hard and required a degree of skill. The other four men were the Roller and the Furnaceman and their assistants.

The Roller was the highest paid member of the team, and was in charge of the mill. The Furnaceman was responsible for supplying the steel at the right temperature at all times. He was often an older man who, for some reason, had not become a Roller. He was always the first to arrive at work, and even before the previous shift had finished he would rake the firebox empty. With a large crowbar he knocked the clinker, or hard slag, from the fire bars. It was hot work, standing by the fire he had raked out. The fire

then had to be shovelled back into the firebox, and be topped up with coal. The bars in the furnace, loaded by the previous shift, could then be prepared for the new shift.

The two assistants were known as the "Bar Dragger" and the "Helper". The fifth man was known as the "Catcher" or the "Aver Over". This was the most physically demanding job of the whole team. He had to catch the hot bars as they came through the rolls, and lifting or levering them back over the rolls to the roller was very hard. As Ike Flavell, the shearer, once said to me, "That aye mon's werk Arch, it's 'osses."

The start of each shift was signalled by the sound of the steam engine starting up, the hissing of steam gradually drowned by the rumble of the large rolls as they gathered speed. Everyone moved to their positions, and took up their tongs, previously dunked in a bucket of water to cool and remove any sweat. The tongs were dunked frequently as sweat made the handles slippery and dangerous.

The furnaceman pulled the first pair of bars from the furnace with short tongs, and dropped them to the floor, on their edges. After giving them a quick rub with a wire brush to remove any scale, the dragger pulled them across the floor to the rolls. The helper caught the opposite end of the bars as they swung towards him, both gave a quick lift, and they were dropped on the plate that sloped down to the mouth of the rolls. The roller pushed the first bar through the rolls, the catcher seized it with his long tongs, and returned it over the rolls, while the second bar was being pushed through. Meanwhile the helper and bar dragger were increasing the pressure on the rolls. When the bars had grown to about a metre in length they were put together and rolled as one until they went through the doubling process.

This was how steel bars were strenuously turned into sheets. Every task in the mill was performed by using a variety of steel tongs, and, after a time, these were used as easily as hands and fingers. Until my hands hardened my palms were almost rubbed raw. The conditions were certainly primitive, and everything around us was made of steel. As someone pointed out to me, "The only thing that can burn in here is the men, and they doh cost much." It was like an oven in the winter - and in the summer it became warmer!

Most of the men took two large bottles of tea to work, and in the summer I would find that I drank between six and eight pints of liquid a shift to prevent dehydration. On afternoon shifts in the summer the holder-down would be despatched to The Bush with a large bag of bottles. I often suffered an attack of cramp, which I now realise was probably due to loss of salt due to excessive perspiration.

These attacks of cramp never took place at work, but would often cause me to leap out of bed and jump around the bedroom shaking my leg. A most embarassing incident took place in a cinema, when I had to move out of a crowded row, hop up the aisle, and perform a dance in the foyer, much to the consternation of a worried looking usherette.

In 1937, and not yet nineteen, I found myself bar dragging in the big mill, and earning more than many men with families to support, but other jobs were now available, and it was time to move on. When passing the site of the works today, and seeing the silent, and rather select, housing estate that stands where the noisy smoke-grimed mills stood, I admit that it is an improvement. But I can still see four men standing round the rolls, each chewing a corner of the sweat cloth around his neck, as the red hot steel moves between them. Like all groups, they had different personalities, but differences were forgotten at work, where we moved as a team. Although not sorry to leave the trying conditions and hard grind of the mills, I was sorry to leave the many friends I made there. Over the years they had truly proved that they were men of steel.

In the following accounts of foundry work you will note that moulders were as pre-occupied with sand as they were with metal. Here is the sand preparation mill at Sandwell Castings in the 1950's. (Black Country Society collection)

The Art of Moulding

Charles Wyatt

I've devoted my life to foundry work, and seen the trade go through great changes, but how I got started in it seems a bit haphazard. I left school in June 1945, and got myself a job in the forge at Adams and Preston's, down in Cradley Heath. I was helping the men who were making ships' anchors. One of my jobs was to fetch their dinner from a canteen, a British Restaurant, about half a mile down the road. Unfortunately I was not really supposed to go off the ground, and one day the gaffer caught me bringing the dinners back. He said, "Yo' can either have your cards, or go in the foundry." I said, "I'll go in the foundry."

I was given a box, pattern, and a great pile of sand, and told, "Yo' can mek them." I didn't know what the devil they were, when I started, nor quite what I was supposed to do, but I found out that I was making the studs to go in chain. I took to it, and did all right with it. I was on 27/6 a week (£1.37½), plus a monthly weight-based bonus which worked out to about £2 or more, on top of my wages. It wasn't bad money so I stayed there until I was sixteen. The Compulsory Works Orders were relaxed at the time, and it was possible for people to leave a job and work where they liked. A cousin of mine got a job at the Simplex, in Oldbury, so I went with him.

I worked at the Simplex, went into the Army, came out, went back to the Simplex, and then got married. While I was at the Simplex I went through all the foundry - starting as a stump moulder, then bench moulding, then foor moulding and machine moulding. Stump moulding was repetition work, working on one pattern plate all day, but the bench moulding was loose pattern work, making one off one pattern, perhaps two off another. Floor moulding produces bigger stuff altogether, and I did that for about five years before going on to machine moulding producing repetition work - "knock-out stuff".

Moulders are generally self-taught. When you start on loose pattern work nobody comes to show you how to do it, so you have to work things out for yourself. Although some blokes would give you a few tips, they are on piecework and don't really have time to help a kid. Nothing learns you quicker than having to find out for yourself, and even if someone showed you how to do something you wouldn't necessarily understand why you were doing it. As far as the firm was concerned, you made a lot of scrap, but, of course, you didn't get paid for scrap - you only got paid for good-uns. You learnt how to run the metal, how to feed it into the mould, and what temperature it should be as it goes in.

We left the Black Country and went to live in Dover. I couldn't get a job at first, but they sent me up to the Dover Engineering Works, which was a foundry making manhole covers - nothing but hard work! When I first went into the office they said they didn't want anyone, until they heard what part of the world I'd come from, and where I'd been working. The manager said, "If you've been working at the Simplex, you can work here - you can start tomorrow! - but what you're gonna do, I dunno!"

When I went the next morning, they gave me a job labouring in the brickyard. After three weeks they brought me into the foundry to help if anybody was away. After a while, if there was somebody away, instead of just helping generally, I would actually take his place - doing his job. In the end I was put on the moulding, and I did about twelve months work before returning to the Black Country, and going back to the Simplex - back on my old job.

Later, one of the foremen at the Simplex started up on his own, in a little foundry at Belbroughton - down among the cornfields. It had been a mill where they had made scythes. I joined him, and his son, and the three of us stayed there about three years until we moved to the Lye and established an aluminium foundry. From wooden patterns we made metal patterns that could be used by the bigger foundries. I started a business with the son, and we went through a couple of moves from Lye to Langley, and eventually to Great Bridge, where we are now. We've been going about eighteen years, and we've seen the processes alter. It all seems different. If an old'un came back now he wouldn't know what to do, or what it's all about.

Working with the sand has changed altogether. When I started we worked with ordinary green sand, and the cores were made of sand impregnated with spermoline, a fish oil that bound the ordinary sand together. Then the cores had to be dried off in an oven for three or four hours, stored and allowed to cool, before use. (The core makers called it "oil-sand", and it was soft when then worked with it, but it was hard by the time we used the cores.) Now we use CO_2 Sand - just ordinary seaside sand mixed with a binder into which CO_2 gas has been introduced. It hardens off very quickly and the core can be picked up and used straight away. In the old days some of the big cores were made around a spit, the sand was mixed with horse manure to bind it together, and, of course, there was great skill in making such cores. The green sand used in foundries usually looks black, but it is red loam sand from Bromsgrove. The old iron foundries mixed coal dust with it that turned it black. Aluminium foundries don't use coal dust, but the continual working of the sand still burns it black - not dirty, just black in colour.

Most moulding work is done by yourself, but when I worked on machine moulding I worked as part of a four-man team - two makers and two casters. And over the years I've worked with iron, with aluminium, aluminium alloys, gun metal, phospher bronze etc... and all these metals have different characteristics. It was useful to work in different foundries, picking up different experience - a good moulder needs time to gain experience and store it in his mind. A lot of people call themselves moulders today, but they aren't real moulders. The real moulder has to know how the metal is going to contract, and to allow for the fact that the thin parts of the casting will cool faster than the thick sections.

In the old days iron foundries used pig iron from places like the Earl's (Round Oak Steel Works), but now a lot of it is imported, but the scrap can still be obtained locally. A 5cwt. charge in a furnace might be a mix of say 3cwt. of pig iron and 2cwt. of scrap, usually called "foreign", plus the limestone to keep the furnace clean. You get your furnace going putting down a bed of thick furnace coke, and then you put your charge on, then another bed of coke, and so on, until the furnace is full. The first charge melts into the well and can be tapped while the next charge is melting down. In foundries the cupolas are often arranged in pairs and worked on alternate days. While you are melting down in the second furnace, you can be clearing the rubbish out of the first.

We don't touch iron now; we only work in aluminium and the yellow metals. Alluminium is a different kettle of fish altogether - the metal is melted down in a crucible inside a small furnace, which is not as hot as an iron furnace. Its more like dipping into a bowl of soup. In the past we used to rely on our eyesight for gauging the temperature of the metal, whereas now we obtain a digital read out. In theory there shouldn't be any mistakes - but there are. Furnaces can be set so that they cut out when the metal is at a certain temperature. In the old days they just kept on running, and thats when you got into trouble - using overheated metal that has "stewed", metal that has had its properties "burnt out", and that has started to go rotten.

Years ago if you had gone to Dudley and Dowell's, and stood by the door, you wouldn't have seen anybody beyond three yards away. It was that dark, dingy, dusty and smokey - you couldn't see the blokes working, but if you go into a foundry today it's that clean you can go to work in your ordinary clothes. The strange thing is that nowadays you have to wear a pair of gloves, because of the resin used in the sand. You wouldn't have seen that years ago, and you wouldn't have been able to mould with gloves on - it was impossible!

There's still a lot of satisfaction in moulding when you've spent two or three hours on one job and turned it out and made a good casting, but it can be soul-destroying. You can work all day, especially on prototype work, and things can go wrong thorugh no fault of your own. The patterns have to be dead right for you to mould off them, but once you've moulded it right - it's great.

Of course, if you put five or six old foundrymen together they talk about old times and set each other off - recalling the funny things that happened. They weren't funny at the time, but talking about it and looking back makes them seem so. This is the kind of thing we would remember: we used to have a chap working with us who wasn't married. He lived with his father so he never used to bring any breakfast or dinner to work with him. One of the dressers had a wooden leg and always used to leave some of his sandwiches in his box at the end of the day. This chap I'm telling you about used to eat the dresser's abandoned sandwiches. One day the dresser left his wooden leg in his sandwich box with a note saying, "Try your teeth on this!".

Joe Ashton

I became interested in foundry work because my father used to work in a foundry. From about the age of ten onwards I took his dinner to work for him, but it was so dark in the place where he worked that I usually had to walk right up to him before I could find him. The roof was very low, and smoke and dust filled the air. If he came home from work and spat into the sink it was black.

My father worked in the iron foundry, but they also had a little aluminium jobbing foundry, where they made ones and twos of things. During the afternoons of my school holidays I stood in there and watched the men at work. They were real moulders - and that's how I became interested.

When I left school, at the age of thirteen, in 1945, my father would not get me a job at Vowle's, so I went to the Bridge Foundry at Wednesbury. I was given a job assisting a chap in the core shop, making cores with black sand, mixing the sand with rope and horse manure to make a mixture that bound together called "muck sand". After about nine months of that, my

Left: Tapping the cupola at T & J's Foundry, Wolverhampton Road, Oldbury, forty years ago. The iron alloy from this furnace went to the foundry to be cast as moulds which were then used in the production of oven-proof glass ware, as well as producing castings for the motor industry. (from "Made in Oldbury")

father relented and I was allowed to join him. He was then working in the alum foundry, and he taught me the trade. He was paid the money that we earned, and he decided how much I should have.

Mother gave me the money to buy a can of tea from the little canteen; one can at lunchtime, and one can at afternoon break. The firm had a slot machine in the canteen - a one-arm bandit, and one lunchtime I put the afternoon tea money into the machine. When the break arrived I told my Dad I had lost the money, which was true in one way, but somebody else told him that I had put it in the machine. He chased me round the foundry with a shovel, and then sent me home. When he arrived home at six he went mad at Mother for not sending me back, and they had a row about it!

I went into the Army from 1949 to 1951, and then returned to Vowle's, but then started work with a floor moulder, making the big stuff. That's when I really began to learn about moulding. Again, it was the moulder who took all the money we earned, and he paid me what he thought I was worth, even though I was now twenty years old. I really did all the work, and he did the braining. That lasted for four years, until the work went short.

They still had a lot of work in the iron foundry, so I volunteered to go back into that, and the money was much better - about £20 a week! After a week's training, I was placed with another volunteer from the alum foundry, and we worked as a two-man team from about 1956 through to 1982 when they closed the place down. For most of that time we made nothing but gear boxes of various sizes for Perkins engines. I learnt a lot about iron, and I saw the process change as the new air-set sand came in. At first the sand would set too quickly, you would be half way through making a big mould, only to find the sand had set like concrete, and there was nothing you could do with it. Nowadays you can control the bench-life of the sand.

Working together as a pair, he made one half of the mould, and I made the other, but I put all the cores in, and he did the labouring part of the job. Eventually

we became a team of four, because we were joined by an Indian guy and a Jamaican. They did the casting while we concentrated on making the moulds. They also took over the knocking out, and mixing the sand.

It was non-stop work in the iron foundry. We walked in at five minutes to seven, took our coats off, and started work, which continued to 12.30., with one ten minute break. While working, the four of us could not even pause to talk to one another. The iron came round on an overhead monorail system, and the moulds had to be ready as the iron arrived. It was piece work, and if you missed your iron, you had to wait for the next lot - losing pounds while you did so! When working like this, my clothes were always wringing wet, especially in the summer. The walls of the foundry were made of corrugated iron panels, and these could be removed in the summer, but it was still hot and dirty.

As the castings were knocked out, the black sand flew everywhere, but later the process was improved and the sand was re-claimed to be sent round to the sand mill. The reclaimed sand could be obtained from the hopper at a push of a button, but sometimes the button was pushed and out would come four kittens - sometimes alive, sometimes dead. Cats used to live in foundries, and often delivered their kittens in the sand hoppers because they were warm. And there were always fleas from the sand to be found in foundries. They tried to improve things by installing extractors, but the dust still collected on top of the ducts. One day you would be working away only to find yourself enveloped in an avalanche of dust from thre duct above you, but you had to go on working.

Although the changes improved the conditions in the foundries, it is interesting that the modernisation killed them off by making them very costly in terms of capital investment, and over-productive. The new plant could make thousands moulds a day, but nobody wants so many castings. Millions were spent on a machine that produced castings faster than they could be sold. The foundries that have survived are the small ones that can make small quantities economically.

Moulders and their sand: Charles Wyatt (left) and Joe Ashton at Charter Castings, August 1990. Joe spreads the air-set sand as it falls from the machine that has blended sand from the hopper above the them with a binder and hardener.

The modernisation had another effect at the same time - it took away the skill of the job. The jobs like knocking out and mixing sand were given to immigrant labour, and some of these men graduated to casting, and eventually to moulding, but, by then, moulding was so mechanised that these men had no chance to learn the skills that we had learned.

When Vowle's closed and I lost my job at the age of fifty five, I found I was fortunate to have learned my skills in the old days, because I was able to get a job at Charter Castings, where the traditional skills are still valued. Making prototypes - perhaps spending the whole day producing a really good casting - is very interesting, and, at the end of the day, it is very satisfying to see the result. I still can't get used to how clean it is now - it's like working in a canteen!

Hopefully I will go on working for some time yet. I am happier moulding now than I have ever been. There's variety in the work, and each job is a fresh challenge. After thirty six years at Vowle's, all I received was my redundancy - but I've been lucky in finding a place where my skills can be used.

Below: Tube making has always been an important industry in the Black Country, particularly in the Wednesbury area, and parts of Walsall and Oldbury. This photograph of Arthur James was taken at Talbot Stead Tube Works, about 1953. Tube mills, like rolling mills, forges and foundries, were noisy and dirty, yet were also places where men established a strong working partnership with the machines.

Making Tubes

Arthur, "Jimmy", James

Because I was a registered furnaceman at the beginning of the War, I found myself working eighteen and a half years on the Pilger Mill at the Talbot Stead Tube Works in Walsall, but it was a strange set of circumstances that brought it all about. My Grandfather had walked from South Wales to Darlaston to work in the local pits, and some years later, when my father found himself out of work he walked from Bloxwich to Yorkshire to work in the pits there. My father died when I was very young and I was sent back to Bloxwich to reared by my Granny.

My mother married again, and started another family in Yorkshire, but I was the eldest, and at thirteen I was ready for work. So they sent for me, and by the age of fourteen, in 1925, I was down the pit at Frickley Colliery in the Yorkshire Coalfield. I expected to spend my life fetching coal, like my Father and Grandfather before me, but a year later, in 1926, we were out on strike, and the strike seemed to go on for months and months. We did eventually go back to work but at the age of eighteen and a half I tried to join the Army as we were only working two days a week at the time. They told me I wor big enough or heavy enough, so I pulled up my tracks and came back to the Black Country in search of work.

I tried to get a job in the pit, but it was bad here as well, and nobody was being set on. In the end I found a job at the Olde Hall Foundry, Revival Street, Bloxwich. I started as a caster's help and worked at

Opposite: Paddy Hogan and Arthur "Jimmy" James, in cap, working as mill hands on the Pilger Mill at the Talbot Stead Tube Works, Walsall, about 1953. Both these pictures were the work of a professional photographer visiting the works, and Arthur had the foresight to ask for a copy for himself.

the place for ten years, progressing through foundry work to the annealing section. In 1938 I was talking to a bloke and he said,

"There's a new factory at Aston. They want some blokes. Yo' am used to heat ay yer?"

"Right!" I says.

Then he says, "Yo'll get 1/3d an hour."

The job I had was paid 1/1½d an hour so I biked it to Aston to get the job. When I come back I went and seen the boss, and asked if I could leave. He says, "Why?"

I says, "I've been offered a job with more money."

"How much?"

"Another three halfpence an hour."

"Oh," he says, "we couldn't pay that." So he gave me my cards and I left.

I started at the new place on Monday and for the first six weeks I was given training. At the end of six weeks they gave a couple of melting pots, and we used to melt swarf, tube ends, anything scrap in aluminium. When we knowed how to melt we were promoted onto alloys - putting copper or zinc into the mix - making a variety of special alloys.

By the time the War broke out I had bought a motor bike for travelling between Bloxwich and Aston, but during the Blackout I drove through a bomb crater and buckled my front wheel. I was forced back onto my push bike as the Army had taken all the motor bikes and spares for their despatch riders! By Christmas 1940 I was determined to find work nearer home. You had to obtain special permission to leave a job, but that was granted, and I started working in the lock trade with my brother-in-law in Willenhall while looking for another job. While I was there a Government Inspector came round and 'ad me.

He said, "We've been after you! You left that firm and we didn't know where you'd gone! This isn't furnace work - and you're a registered furnace mon - so report at the Labour Bureau on Monday." Mr.Reynolds, the gaffer, said, "I tried to keep you, Jimmy, but yo' gorro go - we cor hold yo' cos we've got no furnace here!"

Anyway, I went up the Labour and they told me they wanted to send me to Redditch.

I says, "How am I going to get there?"

He says, "Well, you've got to be there for six because its shift work."

After some argument, he says, "Ave a walk up Bloxwich High Street for a couple of hours."

When I went back he says, "That job at Redditch has been filled, so I am sending you to one at the Spelter - they've just opened a new plant making zinc alloys like mazac, the die-casting metal."

I worked there for nearly two years until the plant was stopped - we had made enough metal to last five years, so we all had to be dispersed. They sent me to a place where zinc was boiled to vaporize it to go in smoke bombs and paint - the place was a real choker, so I told them I was not going in there. The gaffer said, "Yo've gorra learn to do as yo'm told. There's a war on. If yo' cor do that, yo'll have 'ave to go in the Army!"

I was in the Home Guard at the time, and the Army didn't frighten me. I would have been happy to go in the Army rather than that zinc works, but I got sent up to the Labour again. When I went in the clerk said, "Yo' here again! What yo' 'ere fer? I've got just the job for you. Take this Green Card up to Talbot Stead in Green Lane. It's hot work like yo're used to." He wrote, "Heavy Labourer - Hot Mill", on my card - and thats where I went, and I stayed there from 1943 to 1961.

I joined the Hot Mill as a Heavy Labourer but I ended up as the Pilger Driver - one of the top jobs, and I knew that mill inside out. We worked as a gang of nine blokes. The three furnace men were really the top men of the gang, because they had to bring the billet to the right heat, but as the Pilger Driver, I worked the levers on the machine that turned the billets of chrome steel into seamless tubes.

The next step onwards from being Heavy Labourer was to become Spare Mon - capable of doing any job, working the furnace, loading, pulling the billets out with the tongs, releiving any other member of the gang who had to leave the mill to go to the toilet, for example. The work was hot and it was heavy, but I had wrists like iron bands in them days.

We were on the Number Four Mill, producing a tube about every two minutes, or at the rate of twenty five an hour, paid on a piece work basis. But we were left to get on with it without interference. Sometimes the Foreman would just check that everything was going right. He used to say, "Any complaints?"
"Arr," we used to shout, "The bag ain't heavy enough on a Friday."
He'd say, "Same here!", and leave us to it.

I worked closely with Paddy, who had started at about the same time. We used to have a drink together on a Monday morning, and by Monday night we would be fit for duty. We were promoted to Mill Hands and worked our way through each job on the mill. On one side of the mill you could earn a penny an hour more than the other side, and the man who fetched the billet out of the furnace got another extra penny an hour. You had to learn the skill of manouvering the billet into the rolls, putting up with the heat and the black lead dust that got everywhere, and killed a good many with chest diseases. Later you could become the Pilger bar changer, and in the end, I beacme the Pilger Driver. As the driver you had to keep your hands always working and your eyes open - it was quite a responsibility.

During the War we worked eleven hour shifts but after the War we went onto three shifts of eight hours. Working nights during the War was terrible as everything had to be kept shut up, so that we couldn't be seen by Herr Fritz upstairs. He bombed some places near Walsall, and six blokes died when he bombed Bates's plating works, so we had to be careful.

Our mill was the last one to be put down in the works so it was something of a show mill. It was built by Samuel Platt of Wednesbury. I was very sorry see it close down, because, as a team, we got to know it so well, but, of course, all that hand work would be mechanised now. One of the mill hands in our gang was a marvellous engineer. He would bring bits of bikes and motorbikes into work and he would mend them while the tube was being bodged out. He was fantastic - by the time you'd looked at a piece to see what was wrong, he could have mended it - and all in the two minutes it took to produce the tube!

When the mill was closed down I worked at Weldless Steel Tube in Wednesfield, which was also part of the T.I. group, but they would find you jobs like sweeping up, and even that would only last a fortnight. So, at the age of fifty, I had to find "pastures new". I went to Ductile Steel at Short Heath, and was a fitter's mate in the Strip Mill for fifteen years. Now I am retired, and if anybody asked me what I work I'd done, I'd say I was a Pilger Driver - making tubes.

Arthur James died in February 1990, and this account of his career appears with the permission of his daughter, Mrs.S.A.Bate.

Mister Blacksmith

Horace Hodgekiss

I come from a family of blacksmiths. My father and grandfather were blacksmiths, and my grandfather's father owned a company of blacksmiths. My father did not want me to be a blacksmith, but in the thirties there weren't many other jobs around that paid a reasonable wage, so I suppose it was inevitable that it was agreed that I should go into blacksmithing with Dad. Firms were setting lads on at fourteen and then sacking them at sixteen, so my father made the necessary arrangements and, at the age of seventeen, I joined him.

The first few days he let me play about with pieces of steel and the fire - just messing about to get the feel of the fire. At the time we worked with bellows, so I had to learn how they worked, and how to repair them. I would spend a month on one type of work, and then he would move me onto a different kind of work for the next month. It took about a month to become familiar with each job, so that's how it went on for two years.

Then I left my father's forge in Green Lane, Walsall, and went to work for Wheway's. They produced machine made chain, and I went to be their blacksmith, making the tools for their machinists. I made tongs and scrapers, and hardened the tools. I also made shaping and boring tools for the toolroom itself, made in different kinds of materials. I learnt to work with toolroom steel, and learnt to tell one kind of steel from another. As the War came along, my father came to work at Wheways as well.

I was called up, but I only got as far as Walsall station, where I was stopped and turned back. Wheways were undertaking work for the Navy, and I was wanted there. I think I would have rather gone in the forces! At Wheways they were making things that were top secret, so I made fittings without knowing what they were for. (I eventually found out that some were for radar equipment.)

I made some items in monal metal - again not knowing what they were. We sent them off but they were rejected. The boss didn't know why they had been rejected, but I wanted to know, so we tried to find out. Eventually a boffin arrived from Harwell, and he was able to tell me the work had been rejected because the items had skin cracks on them. He said they were to go into an Atomic Pile, and therefore had to be perfectly clear of any cracks. So, in my spare time I practised with the material, and, after a few months, I found a way of working the metal without creating skin cracks.

When I had mastered this I told the firm to get another order - and from then on the orders came in thick and fast, and the company was praised for the quality of the work. Meanwile, my father was still working for me. He was a very clever blacksmith, and a very neat worker, but all his experience had been in working iron and mild steel. Working in stainless steel, and these new materials, was new to him. His health was not good but I knew he was staying on because he was anxious to help me. I asked the firm to give him lighter work, and threatened to leave if they did not. they called my bluff, and I left. My father left a week later. After my departure Wheways could not produce the hooks and tackle in monal metal for Harwell, so they lost that work.

I went to Elkingtons Copper Works to be the blacksmith in their copper foundry. I had to provide the foundrymen on the furnaces with all the things they wanted: hooks, tongs etc. They were just changing over from the one hundredweight pot furnaces to the big rotary furnaces that consumed two tons of scrap copper at a time. They reckoned that if you survived the first fortnight at Elkingtons there was a chance that you might survive a couple of years, which is about as long as anyone ever stayed. Accidents were very common: people tumbled into vats, were electrocuted etc., and the conditions were terrible. But the wages were about four times what they were anywhere else!

All kinds of scrap copper went into the furnace, including some telephone cable in which the coating around the copper had been impregnated with arsenic - to deter animals from chewing their way through the cable. When this went into the furnace, a doctor was in attendance while the furnace was being charged, and when the burners were lit we were evacuated to the other end of the field for an hour or two.

Elkington's perfected a refining process that produced copper that was 99.8% pure, and, at the time, were the only people in the world who could do that. The sludge that was produced as a result of the process contained the gold, silver, iron, and nickle that, in pre-war days had always been the impurities found in copper. The problem was that the fortunes of the firm, and the level of production, was very influenced by fluctuations in the world prices of copper and the ups and downs in the Stock Exchange.

If copper prices fell and production had to be halted, the only way of stopping the process was to sack *everybody* in the copper foundry - even if you were only passing through the place to go to the loo. Usually everybody was re-instated in a day or two, and once the sacked men were reinstated before they had reached the factory gate. At other times production was flat out and anybody could be asked to do anything. At such times, if they had a job that took one hundred hours, they would find one hundred men and do it in one hour!

The experience gained working at Elkington's was valuable, and while I was there I put myself through a gas welding course at my own expense. I stayed there for three years - a lot longer than most blokes stayed. Then a job came up at Elwell's of Wood Green. This time I was going to inspect the working conditions before accepting the job, and, of course, I expected a high wage after working at Elkington's.

The Works Manager showed me the place where I would work: it was a corner of the toolroom. I asked him what he expected me to do, and he showed me a type of tongs they used. I also asked if I could be shown round so that I could gain some idea of whether I would be able to handle their requirements. The Works Manager gave me a tour. I wasn't sure if I was going to take the job but he made up my mind for me! He always called me Mister Blacksmith, and I was treated like Mister Blacksmith.

He told to make the tongs he had shown me, saying that they were short of them. I found out afterwards that this was not true - they were difficult to make and he wanted to put me through my paces. If I could make them, I could make anything! He appreciated a blacksmith, and knew what a blacksmith could do. As it happened, I redesigned the tongs after consultation with the men, and learning how they wanted to hold their work, and after that I found I could often make improvements to production processes, and was sometimes rewarded for my suggestions.

Elwell's tools were first class implements, made of tool steel, they were not cheap things. We were allowed to buy "seconds" at a special price, but after a while we were restricted to buying only what we required for our own use, because local hardware businesses were complaining of lack of sales!

Below: Horace Hodgekiss, Mister Blacksmith, photographed at Elwell's, Wood Green, Wednesbury.

Working at Elwell's extended to doing work for St.Paul's Church, Wood Green, like repairing the clappers of the bells, or providing new rings for their plant tubs, because the church had been provided by the Elwells, who were great public benfactors. They even initiated a special fund that gave us a Christmas bonus, equal to two week's wages, but unfortunately it was not tied to the cost of living, so in the end it became pocketmoney. If you stayed at Elwell's for twentyfive years you werc given a gold watch. I stayed for twenty four and a half years, so the blokes in the toolroom gave me a watch, that I still treasure today.

I spent the last five and a half years of my working life at the North Walsall Bus Depot. A blacksmith was invaluable in straightening out the damaged chasis of any bus that had been in a smash - so I managed to spend my entire working life as a blacksmith.

A blacksmith makes things out of hot metal with a hammer - not that you ever saw a hammer mark on any of my father's work. I liked working with different materials, learning to work them, and being inventive with metal. I did shoe a horse once, but that side of the trade was dying out when I started work. What stayed the same was that wonderful smell of the hearth, of the burning breezes. But what was really satisfying was solving problems, the satisfaction of going home at the end of the day having made some innovation.

Below: Bert Wootton, sheet metal worker, photographed just before his retirement in 1990, after completing over fifty years service at S.J.& E.Fellows, Wolverhampton. (Paul Pickard, Express & Star)

Sheet Metal Work

Bert Wootton

In 1939 I left the Graisley School in Pool Street, Wolverhampton, one Friday, and started work the following Wednesday at the factory next door: S.J. and E Fellows. Starting work as a lad I had to sweep up, fetch the men's work, do a little marking out for the men etc, but I was not allowed to do any real work until I was sixteen. Therc were several other jobs that were regarded as lad's work: like packing items into a railway container to be despatched for enamelling at Barry, or taking pint pot measures, as used by milkmen, down to the Weights and Measures people in School Street, or making acetylene for the welders. Outside the Welding Shop were two big tanks containing carbide. Water used to drip onto the carbide to produce acetylene, and the gas was piped to the welders. Nowaday you just send to the BOC for a bottle!

At sixteen you were supposed to join the union, and you were attached to an older man, someone who had served his time, and you began to learn the job. My progress was halted when I was eighteen and a half by being called up and going into the Army. I served from 1943 to 1947, and on returning to Fellows at the age of twenty two I found I had to start all over again. It was quite a slow process after being away from the trade for four years.

The firm had to allow you to return to your old job, but they were only obliged to keep you for six months, then they could get rid of you if they didn't want you. I certainly did not start work at full rate - 2/7d an hour, I had to work for 2/4d while they decided whether I could do the work - I was fighting for my job!

When I had left the firm there was plenty of work as a result of the War. The firm was making baking dishes, cooking utensils, soya stoves and field kitchens for the Army. After the War everybody wanted their job back just as the firm was struggling to find new products. We were also changing from working in mild steel to working in stainless steel. It was complicated at first, but when I became used to it I found stainless stell was a pleasure to work with. Originally sheet metal workers had not done any welding, but nowadays most sheet metal workers can weld.

I had to crop the metal out from the flat sheet, then build it up, rolling, bending and shaping it, then weld or rivet as required. It was difficult to weld stainless steel with acetylene but argon welding solved our problems. We originally beat articles to shape, but since the War most of that work has been accomplished on presses. At Fellows we also formed by hot stamping - which made the whole place shake. The mild steel items often used to be enamelled, or were tinned in our own shops, but now all that has gone and stainless steel is simply polished.

It took me about two years to feel I was back in the swing of things, and I progressed from day work to piece work, greatly improving my earnings. Sheet Metal Working is a skilled job, and like all crafts it looks easy when you are looking at it, and it is easy for the man doing it, but its difficult to learn. It's a skill that develops with experience. New jobs could often give you a headache, and there was no such thing as producing scrap while you mastered it, so you would often find yourself thinking of moving - but after a week you would be glad you'd stayed!

So many of the products we strived to make are no longer required. We made big two hundredweight aluminium scoops for Avery's - used for weighing coal. We were the only firm around here that could make them because no one else had alluminium welders at the time. We used to make chocolate pans for Cadbury's and Rowntree's. These had to be made very precisely to hold just the right weight of chocolate, but they are not used nowadays. We made galvanised buckets but plastic beat us to that. In the photograph I am engaged in one of our oldest surviving jobs. I am wiring a stainless steel scale pan. I could make about fifty of them a day.

Most people at Fellows lived in Blakenhall, and it was a real family affair. My first foreman, Jimmy Allen, had worked there for fifty years, and his brother, Arthur, worked there, and their father before them. Before I retired several of my colleagues had completed their fifty years of service, including Alf Crockett, Jack Barnes, and Jack Davis. But, as a result of raising the school leaving age, I will be the last to have completed fifty years. Everybody who had worked at the firm since a lad was happy there, but we found outsiders were not so happy.

Over the years we saw the conditions improve. When I started the floor was made of railway sleepers, and you could look straight through the roof, and most of the men in the Press Shop had some fingers missing. There was no sick pay, and there were no pensions until 1957. We worked a 47 hour week.

The sheet metal workers were strongly unionised, and operated a closed shop. We ran our shop. There was nobody breathing down our necks, but there was no slacking, and everybody was expected to do a good job. We did well in order to get ourselves the better paid jobs, and we had a system of working in threes, sharing our earnings if two were on piece work and one was on day rate. Our shop was special, and everybody else waited to see what the sheet metal work shop did when it came to any negotiations.

I believe the firm came from Bilston. Mr.D'Arcy told us that the firm's history went back to the days when the workers had to spend their money in the company's shop, or the company's pub! As times changed the firm had always seemed able to find new products, and that was why I believed I had a job for life. When I started there were still patterns around that showed we had once made milk churns, and as I left the firm was making parts for Japanese microwave cookers. In my time I had seen the number of sheet metal workers fall from twenty five to three, but when I left there were about twelve and work had expanded as a result of making panels for telephone boxes. But sheet metal working is a dying trade, and, in the future, should they want one, they won't be able to find one!

I enjoyed my fifty years, nearly fifty one years really, but I looked forward to retirement and now I'm going to enjoy it. I'm not like one chap who worked for fifty one years and then went back to work another five as a part-timer. I've got two greenhouses full of tomatoes and some fishing to do.

Wednesfield Traps

Ted Tonks

I worked at Sidebotham's trap works in Wednesfield for thirty seven years. It was the last trap works to close, and they have now moved most of it to the Black Country Museum. Mind you, they can't rebuild it exactly as it was - it would be too dangerous! I can remember machines driven by belts that were so low that you had to stoop to get under them. It was quite a primitive place, and most of the workshops had earth floors. Occasionally a building was being demolished and the bosses obtained some second hand bricks with which to brick the floor, but I will always remember it as a hot dirty place with earth floors.

Trap-making was very much a family business - if a father worked there, he would be followed by his sons, and daughters. This was also true for the bosses: the "old man", William Sidebotham, had three sons, George, Harold and Arthur, who all went into the business. There was no snobbishness in those days, and we all lived together in the village of Wednesfield and were involved in the life of the community.

When I was a boy I worked for an electro-plating firm in New Street, but through the Chapel, I got to know Harold Sidebotham. He was a Sunday School teacher, and we started a scout troop and a youth club. About 1924, when I was sixteen, I left the electro-plating shop and went to work for Harold at Sidebotham's Trap Works. I began by doing "odd jobs", and for forty eight hours I was paid ten shillings a week, but the idea was that I should learn all the jobs in the trap trade. When fully trained I would be able to become foreman when one of the elderly men left.

There were two shops at Sidebotham's: one for making "common traps", for export to countries like Africa, Australia and New Zealand, and one for making "best traps", for catching otters and hawks etc., which were sold to the farmers. The "best traps" had brass fittings, so that they could be set underwater if necessary, and they would not rust. Farmers and rat-catchers used to come to the works to buy these traps direct from us.

In the trap trade there are all sorts of jobs that have to be learned, such as forging, hardening and tempering, and we had to be able to work with the old hand bellows for doing intricate work. One rare example of "modernisation" at Sidebotham's was that, if we wanted to do rush work, to forge the big springs that went in the big ovens, we had little blowers to add heat to the breeze on our hearths

To temper the springs, after we had shaped them, and hardened them, we had to take them to a big oven where a dozen were heated at a time. As we put the springs into the oven we dabbed a bit of fish oil on them. The art was not to make them red hot. We would se the flame, and suddenly it would burst - at that point we withdrew the springs and threw them on the floor to cool off.

After they had cooled, we had to test them, to see if they would be able to close the large jaws of the traps. Obviously, we had to be careful when testing traps. Even with the little hawk traps it was possible to trap your own thumbs, and someone would have to come and let you out! On the jaws of the large animal traps there were teeth, and some of the lion traps had spikes rivetted to the jaws as well. We used to make these for Haile Selasie of Ethiopia, and I made the last six dozen exported from Sidebotham's. It took me four months to make them, as all the springs had to be hardened and tempered by hand.

In the big shop, the girls worked on the presses that bent the jaws to shape, and the men generally worked at the benches and forges assembling the traps. Every finished trap was inspected by the foreman. The trap-makers generally worked by their hearths, but one old chap worked an oliver. There was a great deal of skill in making traps, and they had to be just right - even so, they were rough-finished, not all polished up and decorated to exhibition standard. Although it was hard work, I enjoyed it because there was a satisfaction in making something if you knew that it did its job well.

After about eight years I was considered good enough to do "best work", and that's what I wanted to do. They offered me the foreman's job in the "common work" shop, but I turned it down because I wanted make "best traps". It was a good trade to be in. At twentyone I was earning £3.2/6, and a year later I was earning an extra 5/-, which was a lot of money in those days. There weren't many folk earning £3 a week in those days, but we could earn that money by doing piecework, and people in the trap trade kept to themselves.

We earned every halfpence of our wages. We started at eight and finished at six, and never even stopped for lunch. I kept my lunch in my pocket and took a bite when the foreman wasn't looking. After the age of twentyone you were allowed to smoke, but you weren't allowed to keep the cigarette in your mouth. After four and a half hours work on a Saturday I would go to Harold Sidebotham's home in Long Knowle to cut his lawn, after which I was given dinner in his house. Then I would run back to my house, change me, and rush to the football match. Some of the girls, after completing a day's work, went cleaning in "The Smack" - the cinema in Rookery Street, that was looked after by Joe Purshouse, who, by day, was in charge of the Machine Shop.

But we also experienced hard times in the thirties. Sometimes we only worked two days a week, or were laid-off completely for a week. If a small order came in perhaps just three or four men would be called in to complete it. I was on the Means Test for five years. Sometimes work was more likely to pick up during the summer than the winter, especially when rabbits were more numerous. For some reason work picked up just before the War, and during the War itself we made traps for the Ministry of Supply. Traps were catching rabbits and rabbits were food, and if the rabbits were killed off, more food was saved!

I went in the Forces for five years, but after the War, I returned to Sidebotham's for eight or nine years, until I left after a row with one of the bosses. After I left, the trap trade declined, and Mixemetosis finally killed off the trade in rabbit traps. Now we are not allowed to make traps, and the trade has vanished. Yet I can remember the time when we sent rabbit traps out to Australia in their hundreds. They were packed in tanks, supplied to us by the Globe Tank Factory, on Cannock Road, and these were then used in Australia as water tanks.

Wednesfield was once dominated by the trap trade, and by the key-making trade. There was Roberts', of Victoria Road, who made common work, Marshall's in the town itself, and Beech's and Adey's in the High Street, and Henry Lane's, down by the canal bridge, that made exhibition standard traps. People may not like the idea of trapping animals, but rats, rabbits, and even moles, were a pest to the farmer, and our traps did a useful job.

Right: Ted Tonks, on the right, with Harry Craven, both holding the 18 inch lion traps made at Sidebotham's Trap Works in Wednesfield. (Harry Craven was responsible for the press work involved.) The trap works has now been "rebuilt" at the Black Country Museum - but not quite to Ted's satisfaction! The trap making industry of Wednesfield is another Black Country example of local specialisation. (Ted Tonks collection)

Below: As time passes it is becoming more difficult to find local folk who can recall the region's manufacture of motor vehicles, and the associated trades. Examples of the vehicles themselves are being lovingly restored, and books are appearing on the various manufacturers, although the emphasis is still on the glamorous end-products - the cycles, motorbikes, cars etc. Sunbeam, of Wolverhampton, not only produced world speed record breaking cars, but also made aero engines - seen being assembled in this photograph. Later they made machine tools, as described overleaf by Bert Bradford, for the production of components for other manufacturers' vehicles.

Stars and Sunbeams

Bert Bradford

My family had been connected with the cycle and motor vehicle industry since the turn of the century. My father joined the Star Cycle Company in 1894, and was a traveller for them. He travelled all over the country by train, taking one of their push bikes with him to work an area. When motor bikes went into production he had something to do with that, and later he became a director of the Briton Motor Company. The Briton was formed in 1909 by the son of the proprietor of the Star Cycle Company, and were first built in the Frederick Street premises of the latter company. By the First World War the bodies were being built in a factory in Walsall Street.

I was born in Penn Fields, only about a mile from the Sunbeam works at Marston Road, Graisley. I was about five when I began taking notice of motor cars. It was just before the First World War and Sunbeam were considered to be one of the top five car manufacturers. I used to see all the different models when they were out on test. Production of the Briton had moved down to Stewart Street, and my father continued to work for them until about 1922.

After wartime production Star had returned to making cars, and I joined them in 1925, when I left school. At Star they taught me how to use my hands, but first I had to work in the stores and learn all the parts. Their methods of production were pretty backward, as I later discovered, but that didn't matter because it meant that I was taught to use a file and grind a drill etc. Then I went into the machine shop and worked the various machines, and then went into the fitting shop.

About 1928 Guy's bought the Star, and closed the Frederick Street works and moved production to a body-building shop Star had established at Bushbury. I found myself out of work, but found myself a job at AJS. My father was working there by then, and that's how I got the job. I worked in the Jig and Tool Offices at AJS for about three years, learning to be a draughtsman.

Things then went from bad to worse at AJS, so I left and went to Archdale's, in Birmingham, where I began to learn about machine tool design. They were designing the latest types of machines for firms like the Ford Motor Company, so I gained a really good insight into machine tool development. Even so, this was the middle of the Depression, and we were all desperately looking for other jobs, and everybody on my section at Archdale's was put on one month's notice.

Towards the end of that month a rush-job came in, and the boss asked me to try and get it finished by the end of the week. We took the casting drawings out and raced them down to the foundry as fast as we could, and, by the end of the week, the job was more or less completed, just as my notice expired. The boss went to the Archdales, and told them what I had accomplished, so they offered to keep me on, on a monthly basis for as long as there was some work to do.

I had heard about the Sunbeam going into the building of machine tools, so I made a few enquiries, and got myself an interview. Ironically, I was offered a job at Sunbeam just as Archdale's withdrew their notice as they had received a huge contract for machine tools for building Russian tractors! I decided to take the job at Sunbeam.

Sunbeam had set up a "General Engineering Department", using the existing toolroom, foundry, stamp and press shops, but setting out to build things for other people while coming to terms with their own financial difficulties. We made machines for people who had been importers of American and Continental equipment, and who were now inhibited from doing so by new import duties. My machine tool experience was now very useful, and I found myself building some very interesting machines. When I first arrived at the Sunbeam one of my first jobs was to build a lot of jigs and tools for Ford's.

We also made equipment for other people that we had previously made only for our own use, and some of this was quite advanced for its time. One particular item was a camshaft turning attachment for mounting on a lathe. This attachment could turn all profiles of all the cams on the shaft at the same time to very fine limits, and faster than any other machine of its time. I designed one for Rolls Royce, one for Bentley, and about six for the Austin. I still keep a blueprint of it to this day.

Eventually I found myself working at the Austin. I didn't like it there because I was always treated as an outsider. I was assistant to the man who ran the Commercial Vehicle Machine Shop, and on one occasion one of the chaps from the Demonstration Department came over to see him. During the conversation I heard him say that they were having problems adjusting their camshaft turning machines for a new model.
"Do you want a bit of help?" I asked.
"What do you mean? What do you know about it?" he replied.
"Well, I happened to desigm them, and build them at the Sunbeam."
He didn't like that. He was a full-blooded Austin man, and didn't like a whippersnapper telling him what to do.

While I was at Sunbeam we also built many machines for Alexander Machinery, who were the well known importers of nut and bolt manufacturing machines. We did so well that Alexanders bought that side of the business and moved it to a new plant established for such work at Dudley - at Waddams Pool, when Sunbeam closed. A lot of people from the Sunbeam went to work there, but I didn't like the idea of doing so. I did a little tooling for the last car that Sunbeam made: the Dawn, which came out in 1934. Car production ceased the following year. A subsidiary of the Rootes group took over the Moorfield Works, and Guy's took over the commercial vehicle production (trolley buses). I found myself another job and sadly ended my interesting association with Sunbeam.

The twists and turns of my career still took me back and forth between Wolverhampton and Birmingham. After working for several Birmingham firms, I did return to Wolverhampton for a time to work for Henry Meadows who were acquiring machine tools from America on the Lend-Lease scheme during the Second World War. History repeated itself for me in Wolverhampton, because after the War, Henry Meadows fortunes declined, and I returned to Birmingham in search of work. I eventually worked for twenty five years with a machine tool firm called Wilcox, where I became a director.

I liked the development of machine tools in the days before computer control. And I like the machining itself. The feel of a machine is beautiful. If only you can get your hands on a lathe - on the hand wheels and the knobs - it's a lovely feeling, like eating strawberries. I think I first discovered that when I worked at the Star, because that is where I first worked on a lathe. I made a lot of mistakes including scrap, but I learned how to do it, and I do think that some people have an instinct for working on machines, just as other people have a natural ability to do other jobs. I have always loved making things on machine tools.

I would have loved to have equiped my own workshop, but I would never had time to work in it, as I had many other interests. I was a big poultry keeper at one time, and a keen gardener. For twenty five years I grew and processed my own tobacco. It was grown on my plot on the allotments by Jeffcock Road - owned by the Graisley Co-operative Allotments Association, and I spent two nights a week processing it. Even non-smokers liked the smell of my tobacco. I smoke the best tobacco I can get, but its not as good as the tobacco I made myself. I put a great deal into the development of that tobacco, and I suppose that's what I like doing. I like experimentation and development of things - whether its processing tobacco or machine tools.

Below: Seated in the foreground is Vera Hodgekiss inspecting shell cases at Kynochs. Vera describes how girls from Walsall responded to the need to undertake munitions work during the last War. (Vera Hodgekiss collection)

Munitions Work

Vera Hodgekiss

When War broke out in September 1939 I had been working as a baster at Edgar Stammers for four years that had passed since I had left school. At the time I wanted to be a nurse, and had already obtained some qualifications in that direction. My Father was totally opposed to the idea. "You will be sent abroad during the War, and I'm not having that," he said. I felt that I had to do something to help the War Effort, and in defiance, without asking my parents or even letting them know, I arranged an interview at Kynoch's, the munitions factory at Perry Bar.

When I arrived for the interview I joined a lot of other girls all in a line. We were taken into the offices, and I was astonished to find that we had to line up, about twenty of us in the row, with our backs to the wall.

A lady appeared, who seemed "elderly" to me at the time, with long earings and a very stern look. She came along the line and looked us up and down, turned us round, turned us back and sideways. I couldn't understand why, but apparently she was looking for the type of girl that she wanted for a particular job. I kept on thinking to myeslf, "I hope she doesn't pick me," because I didn't like the look of her - but she did! I must admit that all my assumptions about her were wrong, and that she was a very nice lady to work for.

We started the following Monday, working from eight in the morning until six at night, which meant that I had to be out of my house by seven in the morning and that it would be seven o'clock at night before I returned to my home in Walsall. On that first morning I did not even know what kind of job I was going to be doing.

We were taken into a long room - like a huge garage with doors at each end. In front of us were rows of examination tables, and I had to start work as a feeder. I had to stand on a board, propped up by a high stool, and had to feed the bullets onto a slide that took them passed the inspector after I had arranged them so that they were all facing in the same direction. I plunged my hands into the box of rather greasy tracer bullets. "Oh dear", I said as I found myself looking at them. The girl who was the examiner, said, "Vera, you've got to get used to getting your hands dirty!"

"I'm not worried about that," I said, "I feel sick because some of these bullets may kill someone." I remember that moment very well, and it did make me feel sick that morning, but one gradually got over such things.

After working in that room for about twelve months we were told that preparations were being made for the work to be done in a new, more modern, place, a big department where we would still be doing the same kind of job. When we moved into the new room I was given the job of leading examiner, which made me feel proud as it meant that my work was good. As leading examiner, the bullets came down my slide, between rows of mirrors in which I could see the heads and tails clearly. I rolled them down to inspect the body of the bullet, looking for flaws, such as cracks in them. The faulty ones were thrown into a box, and the ones that passed my inspection dropped into a hopper. Two overseers constantly walked up and down, checking our work, before the hoppers were loaded into trucks. When the truck was full, which could take a morning's work, it was taken away to be weighed, and you were then paid piecework on the weight you ahd turned out.

I stayed in the Inspection Department for a long while, working up to eighty one hours per week - I wish I'd kept one of my time cards to prove it! We had to work Saturdays and Sundays, and it was in that time when the War was going very badly, and there were shortages of ammunition. Harry Webb told me that he was very satisfied with my work as leading examiner, and ability to set the pace for the other examiners. He asked me if I would like to move to another examining point - inspecting large cases. I transferred to this work, and again spent about twelve months doing it. We had happy times doing these jobs, but as an examiner, I always had to bear in mind what Harry Webb had said to me: "Now Vera, remember that if you pass faulty work it can backfire on our own boys." I had to live with that thought, and made sure I always did my work well.

As the hours started to get longer, we were asked to work two weeks on a day shift, and two weeks on nights, on twelve hour shifts. This was very tiring, and when working nights I went pale, lost weight, and went off my food. As a newly-wed I would have to come home and climb into a warm bed that my husband had just left! One brighter aspect of working nights was the long trip to the canteen. Whatever the weather it was good to get out of the workshop, and about twice a week, a variety show was put on to entertain us between one and two in the morning as we had our break.

Lots of the girls from Walsall used to catch the same buses to get to work. We were expected to be in our unit by eight o'clock in order to clock-on. although we could be passing the gates at eight o'clock, it was impossible to reach our department until two or three minutes after. The Under-Foreman used to travel with us from Walsall, and, strange as it may seem, it was him who reported us for being late.

Mr.Webb called us all into the office, and said, "I'm sorry about this, and I know it's hard on you, but you have got to be here before eight." Some of the girls protested that it would be very difficult. He went on, "It doesn't matter how difficult it is, you've got to do it." They all agreed they would try - all, that is, except Vera!

As the Under-Foreman was in the office with us, I said, "Mr. Webb, although I don't know how I can manage it, I will do my best. as long as he does the same, because he travels on the same bus as us!" This seemed very outspoken for a twenty-year old girl, but Mr.Webb simply turned to the Under-Foreman and said, "Can you manage it?"

"Oh Yes, I can do it all right."

When I heard that I said, "Well, I'm not going to make any promises. In fact I don't think I'll even try because I am positive it can't be done with the buses timetabled as they are."

"Before you leave this office, Vera," said Mr. Webb, "I've got to tell you that if you do not comply, you will have to be suspended for three days."

"Well Mr. Webb, you'll have to supend me for three days, but if you do I shall take three weeks!"

"You can't do that - we'll have to put you in for a summons - you may well end up in court." That's how it was during the War.

As he could make no progress with me, he picked up the phone and arranged for me to be sent to the Personnel Officer. Once again, she insisted that I be there for eight, but I told her that I could not promise to do that. "And are you going to take three weeks if we suspend you?"

"Yes I am!" - and I did. And I lived through hell for three weeks, terrified to go to the front door in case a summons was waiting for me. I felt awful, but I stuck it out.

When I returned to work I walked striaght in to my position - but there was another girl doing my job. She said, "Sorry Vera, but you' lost your job." I stood there while she carried on working until Mr.Webb spotted me from his office window. He sent the Foreman down to fetch me up to his office.

"Well Vera, you did it didn't you? You know you've lost your job don't you?"

"Its unfortunate, but I still have a clear conscience. I cannot get hear for eight o'clock."

"No, and nor can any of the others! You were quite right, so we owe you a sincere apology. Now, how would you like to come and work for me personally as a Quality Controller? You have the initiative and guts to do it."

"Well," I said, "its worth a try."

He sent me home for another week, and I started the following Monday in C Case, an extremely large department. Mr. Webb took me in and took me up to the offices, up on a gantry above the shop floor. We stood at the rail and had a chat. It was quite a shock because the place was so vast. Big machines were bumping away in the distance, and small lathes were working nearer to us. He put me into a lovely white overall - just the right size - and we walked along the floor, between white lines that marked out the gangways.

He said, "You are walking very straight with your head high. Can I give you a bit of advice? Keep it that way! Your job is going to be very difficult, and you will have to ignore the jibes. Men, in particular, will not like you telling them to stop their machine, even if it is turning out faulty work."

I had to learn to use the micrometer, and then it was my job to go to each machine and check its output, and fill in the quality control cards at the back of the machine. Jibes were directed at me, and the men made passes, and the married men were always asking me out, but after a while I was accepted. There was one other lady quality controller but she was much older than me.

At Kynoch's we were never allowed to know too much, and it was such a large place that it was impossible to know what was going on everywhere anyway. When we passed through the main gates, in our hundreds, so many would be stopped and searched to see if we were taking anything dangerous home. I was stopped only once, and I did not like it, I can assure you. We were pulled into side rooms, and had to strip down to our underclothes, and were searched thoroughly.

Sometimes I had to go onto the Danger Field, through another set of gates, but you were generally trusted if your work took you into that area. You could hear firing going on where bullets were being tested, but you never wandered away from where you were supposed to be going. I did have a shock the first time I went over there. I passed a line of huts with no doors on. Inside I could see girls knee-deep in powder, some were up to their waists in it. In C Case we sometimes had to walk through the slurry from the machines, but I realised I should not grumble about the jobs I had to do.

Some people worked in dangerous conditions. For example, on one ocassion, a man fell into a vat, and was killed. And when the sirens went we had to make for the nearest shelter. One night I found myself in a shelter, only separated by a narrow alley way from a huge gunpowder magazine. If they had dropped anything we would have been blown sky high. Barrage Balloons above the works usually protected us during the air raids. Another upsetting fact of life was the death of a colleague in the raids on Birmingham. A girl called Vera, the same as me, was drowned in her shelter one night, and it was three days later before they dug her out and found her children in her lap.

Despite upsetting times, the long hours, and sometimes the danger, we did have happy times, particularly in that canteen, and we made many good friends. I don't remember any bitchiness or bickering - we just got on with the work. As the works was in Perry Bar, and stretched right through to Witton, the workforce was recruited from both Birmingham and Walsall, but there seemed to be far more from Walsall than Brummies. Eventually we were told that it was because we were better workers - and we worked at a cheaper rate! (Not because we wanted to - but because they could get us for a cheaper rate.)

When I had informed Stammers that I was leaving to go and work at Kynoch's, they said, "Silly girl! The War will be over by Christmas. Go if you must - but you'll be back in your old job after Christmas." But - I wasn't; I worked at Kynoch's throughout the War, for about five years.

The Rivet Heater

Cecil Westwood

Having never had a secondary education, I find myself looking back to the elementary training we were given at Rowley Regis Church of England School. Nothing was added to our lessons in the way of recreation like you might find today. Our only break from the lessons were a few minutes morning and afternoon when we were allowed to go onto the hard rough ground until we heard the headmaster's whistle calling us back to our classes. Some of the boys, including myself, returned with the backs of our hands a little grubby as a result of playing marbles - "Chuck - a'-th'-'ole" etc.

I don't know how, but I passed standard seven, and left school in 1919 at the age of 13. One or two were admitted to Wright's Lane School, Old Hill, for further education, and, in those days, unless you had attended Wright's Lane, there was little parents could do in arranging a job - it was just a matter of finding "anything".

I applied for a job at a local nut and bolt factory, where one of my friends who had also left school at 13 later became Chief Buyer. I found myself joining some other lads in the bar shearing department, doing a job known as pin-stacking. Perhaps this is worth mentioning, because I understand that this type of job no longer exists.

After the bars of steel had been sheared into various lengths, to be headed into a bolt, there was a niche or cut left at the end of the pin created by the shearing. This caused the pin to be irregular, and if this end was put down into the hole of the die of the heading machine it may well have become stuck. The pin-stackers stood at bins raised to the correct level for lads to operate. The bins looked like market stalls. Our job was to pick up the pins and place all the same way on trays - the nicked end being in the correct position, so that the heaters (usually older people) could push them into the furnace holes, using tongs, and throw them out to the operator of the bolt machine. The right end was thus heated ready for heading, and later screwing. The lads became quite deft with their fingers and could fill a tray with these small pins in a very quick time.

Later the lads would move on to other more significant jobs in the factory, but I left before making any progress. I know people who spent all their working lives at T.W. Lench Ltd, but I listened to a pal of mine who told me his uncle could get me a job at the Metropolitan Carriage & Wagon Works, in Oldbury, as a rivet heater. My pal and myself presented ourselves at the gatehouse of our new employer.

The gatehouse was also the time office, and we were given a piece of metal - a fairly thin metal sheet measuring about eight inches square. This was a time sheet, on which our hours were written in chalk. Plates still in the time office after starting time were an indication that there were absentees. Later time clocks were introduced but when we started the plates were still in use. The man in the office asked, in a friendly way, if I was related to another Westwood that he knew via Methodist connections - and that was my father.

We walked along the drive to the Frame Shop,

where large hopper wagons were standing. They had been put together with a nut and bolt here and there to hold the plates in position until the many holes had been filled by the riveters. The work was done by teams consisting of a riveter, a holder-up, and a rivet-heater. My friend was taken off to another part of the factory where, I think, they were making carriages for the East India Railway, but I was led over to two men, and the riveter said, "Are you the new rivet lad?"

Within a few hours his mood had changed. If patience is a virtue, this man did not possess such an attribute, and certainly he found it difficult to tolerate anyone who was new to the job. I was unable to cope with the breeze fire, which needed constant attention with a poker, lest it fell into the hole around the tyrere from which came the blast from an electrically driven fan. The rivets varied in length, being placed round the hot spot of the fire, and gradually worked in rotation to the middle. If the fire fell into a hole, the rivet fell through and was lost around the tyreree. Apart from this, one had to remember which rivet was needed next. The riveters said they wanted the rivets to come "looking like a bit of butter", but I must have been handing them to him either too hot, or not hot enough, or with the ends burned.

The holder-up was fairly neutral. His job was to hold the dolly up against the existing head, having placed the heated rivet through the hole with his tongs. Even so, his job was made more difficult if the rivet was not correctly heated. I was surprised that such a job was given to a new lad, and had always understood that such work was done by experienced men in the shipyards - men who could throw their heated rivet from their tongs a long distance to arrive at the feet of the riveter.

I suppose there were good rivet heaters and bad ones, and I feared that I might be one of the latter, but practice produces improvement. Funnily enough, about ten years later my wife and I met this riveter in Tividale. He remembered me and told my wife what a good rivet lad I had been! Good for him!

Sometimes a rivet had to be sheared off. Occasionally an inspector would come round, and with a small hammer, he would gently tap the riveted head. If it had a certain sound it was ringed with chalk and the head had to be chopped off. Sometimes this would be discovered before such inspection, and, without wasting words, the riveter would call for the sett - a heavy chisel used by blacksmiths. The riveter would hold the edge of the sett against the head of the rivet, and the holder up would apply a few sharp blows, and the faulty rivet would be removed. The sett was always kept handy - usually under the hearth. One day a group of us was walking through Oldbury town on our way to work and we passed a paper boy selling Birmingham Gazettes. He was shouting something that sounded like, "'Zette", and a well-known riveter from Blackheath shouted back, "It's under the ---- hearth!"

When the hopper wagons were completed we were stopped and I found myself unemployed. I had not been out of work too long, when a Mr. Siviter, came to our house to say I was wanted back as another order had come in. This time we were making ordinary trucks rather than hoppers, but they had floors that had to riveted onto a frame of light girder work. The frame-fitters placed the steel sheets on the girders leaving hundreds of holes to be filled with rivets.

The holder-up had to sit underneath the frame and receive the hot rivets thrown to him. In this situation he used a short dolly, and after pushing the rivet through the appropriate hole, he wedged the dolly up against the rivet and the inside of the girder. He had to sit with his legs astride a piece of tin onto which I threw the hot rivet. One day I threw one which went up his trouser leg. He came out faster than a whippet - fortunately without being burned.

On this job the rivets were mainly of a standard size, and therefore they did not need to be heated in an open fire. An iron plate, with many holes, was placed over the fire, and the rivets were just dropped through. this made the job easier for the rivet heater - and if a rivet was burned it was not passed on to the holder-up because it just would not come out of the plate. If too many were burned the number of holes would drastically decrease and I would have to find another plate. Another disadvantage was that the state of the breeze fire below the plate could not be seen, and was liable to fall into a hole if one did not continually lift the plate to feed and tend the fire.

Even so, this kind of rivet heating was regarded as "chicken feed" compared to the skill required to hide a dozen rivets in an open fire wihout losing one, and always bringing the centre one out "like a bit of butter", continually working from the outside to the centre and producing the right length rivet at the right time. During this second phase of work I worked with George Harold - one of three Whiteheath brothers who all became riveters. He was a very patient man and I think we respected each other.

After this order was finished we were again stopped, and I never returned to the Wagon Works. The premises themselves were later taken over by another firm. I worked for another fifty two years until retirement.

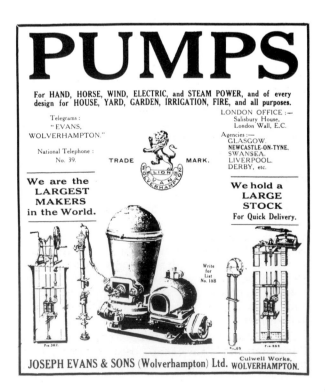

The Culwell

Cecil Perry

Joseph Evans & Sons, of Heath Town, Wolverhampton, was known locally as "The Culwell". Established in 1810, its principal business was the manufacture of hydraulic pumps, and its world-wide reputation was built upon traditional Black Country engineering skills.

The Culwell Works occupied a sprawling site clearly identified by its tall square chimney stack with the name, EVANS, on its sides. With a workforce of about two hundred, it had its own foundry, pattern shop, forge, smithy, machine shops, and pump test facility, plus, of course, design/drawing office, sales and publicity and administration functions.

When I joined the company in 1944 as an indentured apprentice, the metal-cutting machines (lathes, planers, millers, etc.) were still operated by belting from overhead shafting. The prime-mover was a large electric motor, but back-up power was provided by a gas engine or a vertical quadruple cylinder steam engine.

The pumps were literally hand-built in the fitting shops, the components being filed, scraped and/or bedded in, and the workmanship was a source of pride in the company. Keyways were often hand-chiselled, filed and scraped, and keys were hand made.

The pumps varied from the old village type, with fluted columns and swan-neck levers, to enormous motor-driven horizontal triple ram units. Some of the latter were used to pump oil from England to the Normandy beaches under "Operation Pluto" ("Pipe Line Under The Ocean"). Large vacuum pumps for use on whalers were impressive by the size of their tall jar-shaped chambers. They were made of cast-iron in our own foundry, and a quality check consisted of striking them with a large hammer to check that they rang like a bell. The company was particularly well-known for its range of steam pumps, steam then being a common source of power in gas works, mines, chemical plant etc.

The "Cornish" steam pump used a combination of sliding spools in a steam chest to provide the alternating supply to either side of the cylinder - no external linkage, or mechanism, being required. This was the "Black Magic" of its day, and the knowledge used in their construction tended to be handed down from engineer to engineer, the manufacturing drawings being somewhat inadequate. Another popular range was the "Reliable", using a traditional crankshaft, flywheel, kite, and slide valve. As an apprentice, it was an anxious moment to witness the application of steam into a pump for the first time, having built the pump oneself "from scratch".

However, it was the double expansion beam engine steam pumps the captured the eye and ear, with their hypnotic rhythmic oscillating motion, clicking of the mechanical lubricator, swish of the slide mechanisms, slurp of the rams through the pump glands, and overall, the sibilant hiss of steam. I recall with sadness that one of these lovely examples of British craftsmanship finished up on the bottom of the Atlantic - victim of a U-Boat.

An unusual pump, providing "something for nothing", was the "Ram" pump - used for forcing water from a stream to a local house. It used the kinetic energy of the flowing water to charge an air reservoir, and then eject a quantity of water up to a storage tank. Even today you may hear the steady "thump - thump" of such a pump, possibly deep in a wood.

The drawing/design office was a far-cry from today's high-tech facility. Drawings were created on thick cartridge paper, using very hard 6H pencils, and Indian Ink for dimensions and lettering - no room for error. Tracings were then made onto coated Irish linen, and ammonia prints taken from them. The print machine was an archaic governor-controlled carbon arc lamp type which descended into a swivelling cylindrical glass case.

Perusing some of the old drawings provided fascinating glimpses of the activities of our engineering forefathers. I remember coming across one drawing of a deep-well pump, shown at the bottom of a shaft. The bricks, and mortar of the shaft were clearly drawn and even the moss and lichen were lovingly shown! The steel spindle driving the pump was shown, attached to a turntable in the farmyard. The draughtsman had completed the picture with a horse, some chickens and a barn! The dimensions of the pump carried the note, "measured from existing pump" - in other words it was a case of make it first, and draw it afterwards.

Memories of working at "The Culwell" at that time come flooding back. I remember the creosote-soaked railway sleepers that formed the floor in the fiting shop where I worked, the oily brown scarred finish of the old lathes, the billy can of water for tea always on the boil over an illicit gas flame in a discreet corner. And, of course, I remember the camaraderie, and our pride in the company's products, bearing the rampant lion trademark.

The beginning of the end occured in the late 1940s, when the company was swallowed up by Newman Industries. The old ways and anachronisms could not survive in the Post-War era. It has long-gone, but the skills and knowledge that I learnt there stood me in good stead in my subsequent career. I am proud to have been at "The Culwell".

Goodyears and Best Years

Alf Bridgwood

When I left school in 1913, I went to work at the Cannon and I stayed there for twenty six years, apart from four years in the Army. I was called up in 1917, and returned to the Cannon early in 1922, to be a moulder. It was a terrible job - casting gas stove components in slave labour conditions. It was awful but I expected to stay there for life.

In September 1939 I had a row with the foreman and walked out. If he had called me back before I left the yard I probably would have stopped - that's the way we used to accept the job we were doing. Even though I didn't like the work it's amazing how I became attached to the place after twenty six years.

I was lucky - I started work at Goodyear's the next day. I had a brother who worked there and he spoke for me. The Second World War was imminent and they had just opened a new department. Facing the

Above: Alf Bridgwood in the Hose Department at Goodyear's factory in Wolverhampton, July 1956. Sixty foot lengths of hose had to be cured and blown off the mandrel. Finished hose was been passed to the girls at the table in the background for inspection. (Alf Bridgwood collection)

Above: Alf Bridgwood testing the flow of current through the wire embedded in petrol hose, July 1956. The man who used to sing at the top of his voice is still a good storyteller and joker - and didn't really want to talk about work at all - that's why he has been given the last word!

prospect of a shortage of labour, they were willing to take on someone who was too old to be called up. I was offered 1/3d an hour - ten shillings for an eight hour day. I was put in the new shop opened to build hose pipes, which became a very essential part of War-time production. If we hadn't made the hose pipe we would have lost the War! Hose pipe isn't just made so that folks can fill their kettles; it was made for all sorts of purposes, and we made pipe up to 24 inch inside diameter.

I was repsponsible for curing the hose pipes. The hose was built in sixty foot lengths and arrived at my bench all bandaged up. They were built on mandrels, and it was our job, after they were cured, to remove the bandages and get the hose off the mandrel. The hose had to be blown off the mandrel with compressed air, and they were then passed to the girls who did the inspection work. I could pick up a hose while it was still hot because I was used to handling hot things. I was used to a hot environment, but it could also be steamy and wet, and there were duck boards on the floor. I was first hand in a four man team. I worked with three Polish chaps, one of which used to call me "Father"!

I did a few other jobs. For example, I made Turks Heads for the Admiralty - they were rubber fenders, three to a twenty foot length of rope, and there was an art in making them neatly. I also worked on the petrol hose. This had to have a continuous thread of wire running through the wall of the hose. My job was to expand the wire into the rubber, and after curing, check that the current could flow from one end of the hose to the other. While doing that work, I had my back to a machine that made a colossal noise. I used to sing all day at the top of my voice, and I

think they used to think I was talking to myself until one day there was a power failure and the machine stopped while I was singing at full volume. Although I applied to leave the Hose Department several times, they would not let me go as it was hard work and nobody else wanted to do it. After I retired the work was transfered to their factory in Belfast.

The strange thing is I stayed there twenty six years once again - until I retired in 1965. And now I've been retired for almost twenty six years, but I'm not packing in yet - I want to live to get a telegram from the Queen. At my British Legion club I'm the only one left who served in the First World War.

My four years in the Army were the best four years of my life. I went to France and when the War finished I re-enlisted. When we came back to Liverpool in 1919 we were sent in to break a Police strike. I wouldn't have liked to be a policeman in Liverpool - we soldiers had to walk around in fours for safety! But then I went out to India, and while I was on the ship on the way there, I entered a boxing tournament. When I arrived in India I was put in the Boxing Team, and ended up touring India in the physical training team. I had a really good time.

Everywhere I went I met lads from Sedgeley - I don't know what the Army would have done without Sedgeley. And I usually managed to arrive on the scene when conflicts were coming to an end. Even at Christmas 1921, I landed in Southampton expecting to return to Sedgeley on leave, but they took us over to Ireland instead. As we got there a truce was signed, so I was demobbed, and that was when I retuned to the Cannon.....There you are: we've ended up talking about work again. I'll tell you, if we could stop ourselves talking about it - it would probably go away!